THE
CROFT
AND·THE
CEILIDH

THE
CROFT
AND·THE
CEILIDH

Gideon Scott May

With Sketches By
SANDY CHEYNE

The Melven Press

Perth 1981

Published by
The Melven Press,
176 High Street, Perth, Scotland.

ISBN 0 906664 08 X

Printed in Scotland by
Bookmag, Henderson Road, Inverness.

*I dedicate this book to Irralee
who has so lightheartedly shared
life at Croft Douglas and laughed
or cried whilst typing each chapter.*

1

Have you ever had a dream so real, an experience that did not fade on awakening, something that you felt just had to come to pass?

One night I found myself in a field full of fat lambs, of cattle munching their way, with rhythmic contentment, through the clover-studded pasture; in a farmhouse, snug, solid and serene, surrounded by a wooden fence held together with a mass of rambler roses.

Next morning I had to tell someone, and who more understanding than the girl I had married? Irralee has the name of a river and the bubbling, easy-flowing temperament to go with it, she also has a great passion for horses and her first query was, 'had I seen a paddock for a pony?' Together we shared the excitement of the search, and the disappointments, too, until, one day Irralee came running towards me waving a copy of *The Courier* wildly above her head.

Words poured from her like machine-gun bullets. She always speaks this way when excited and, most confusing of all, back to front! Translation takes time and tries Irralee's patience to the limit. But yes, the picture of a Highland farmhouse did bear resemblance to the image we had now set our hearts on. So we tumbled, along with our three little girls, Maureen, Valerie and Gillean, into our car and set off with high hopes for the Road to the Isles.

It was a day fit for the occasion, the sun was warm on the backs of our necks, lighting up the windows with a friendly glow. The bumble bees were having a party and staggered in and out of the roses, waving their forelegs in a tipsy welcome.

We looked up to the silver birches and the purple bell heather behind the house, then turned around to view the lush pastures sweeping down to the blue waters of Loch Tummel and turned again to hug each other in delight.

At my feet was a molehill freshly thrown up. I knelt down

and dug my fingers deep into the sandy earth and grasped a handful. I opened my fingers and watched the earth run through, the particles of mica glinting in the sunshine. Who, I thought, ever discovered gold quite like this? It had to be ours and, in no time at all, we called Croft Douglas home.

We bought our first milk cow and her calf, and poultry for the henhouse. The roses were dying now, a sure sign of coming winter, so we also purchased a load of turnips and potatoes, some corn for the hens and a stack of hay. After all this, a glance at our bank book revealed that we had £40 to see us through the long months of winter. But we consoled ourselves, for we had milk, butter, eggs, turnips and potatoes, fish from the loch and I glanced at my gun in the corner. I never liked to shoot for shooting's sake, but when necessity knocked that was a different matter. Little did I realise how often Daddy would have to go a-hunting.

A few days after laying in our winter 'stores' I fell to temptation by going to the market. I don't know how it happened as I had never had anything to do with pigs and didn't particularly like them, but there was a poor fellow driving a huge Wessex sow round the ring, and at each turn he looked more disconsolate as the auctioneer tried to cajole bids from the crowd. Eventually, with shoulders hunched and shaking his head, he took the sow from the ring with the auctioneer chanting,

"Thirty-nine, come, gentleman, is there any advance on thirty-nine?"

I somehow got talking to the little man, who assured me that the sow was worth at least £60, that she was imminently expecting a litter, and that he didn't want to take her home as there was no room for her there. I commiserated with him and, to my surprise, he turned and asked,

"Would you like her?"

"My worldly wealth only amounts to £40," I replied.

"You can have her for that."

Considerably shaken, I found myself with an empty bank book and Arabella.

I was halfway home before the enormity of what I had done smote me between the eyes. I had squandered our carefully saved 'living money'. What was I going to say? Money had never gained my respect. I hated what it did to people, and considered it the root cause of most of the disturbances in a troubled world, but things were different now. I was married with responsibilities.

Casually, over tea, I mentioned that we had a Wessex sow coming from the market. Irralee took it quite well and I decided to skip any details for the present. But the sow didn't come, so, full of apprehension, I made my way to the nearest 'phone box and contacted the carrier, only to be told that he had hunted the entire market and couldn't find the pig!

"What did it cost?"

The dreaded question stung me between the shoulder blades as I reached for my coat.

"Everything", I gulped and disappeared into the night.

How ghostly the market was now, as I listened to the ringing echoes of my footsteps on the cobblestones. Up and down the dimly-lit alleyways, my heart sank lower and lower as I peered in vain into the dark corners of empty pens. Nothing, save the sleepy whisperings of roosting sparrows.

Suddenly, a huge black shape bounced up in front of me. The shriek of a tormented chain set my teeth chattering and I found myself gazing into two fire-flecked eyes set in a matt of hair. But I had only disturbed a bull who was 'Bed and Breakfasting', and was just as startled as I. I wandered out into the yard, where the tang of the meadow hay met me. I followed it to a half-open door. Inside, I fumbled down the wall for a light switch, found it, and there, her huge bulk spread luxuriously across the hay, lay Arabella.

Eventually, I got her home and spent the next two nights popping in and out of bed, checking to see if she was alright, and panicking at her every tummy rumble! On the third night exhaustion caught up with me and dealt a knockout blow. I came to with a start, my first thought — I hadn't seen Arabella for at least six hours! I heaved on my coat, lit the hurricane lamp and went out, shivering, into the cold night.

There she lay, acres of pork in the lamplight, and not a care in the world. It was then it happened. With a great sigh, a little kick of the hind legs and a series of soft grunts, like some machine disgorging an assembly line of pre-packed goods, Arabella went into production. I was flabbergasted. The whole operation took on a military aspect as each package tore asunder and a tiny, squeaking object paraded in a tottering semi-circle round the sty to take up position on that mountainous flank. One, two, three, four, five, six times! Seven, eight, nine, surely this can't go on. Ten, eleven. The perspiration dripped from me. A large ear wiggled. Thank goodness, I thought, that must be the 'All Clear' signal. I tiptoed shakily from the scene. Arabella, magnificent in her maternity, grunted contentedly, and the long line of piglets wriggled and squeaked. A little mouse, scuttling along an overhead beam, sat up and rubbed its eyes. I rubbed my eyes too.

The piglets flourished and, when able to tackle an additional diet of boiled potatoes, laced with lashings of cow's milk, grew like mushrooms. I counted the days until they would be big enough to go to market, for inside the house it was another matter. The Croft Douglas table was more than bare. I reached to take the cover off the inevitable dish of eggs and potatoes which, no matter how disguised, tasted like eggs and potatoes. Trying to take the family's mind off the monotony of eating the same thing day after day, I brightly spun a story of my shady ancestors who had earned the name of 'Bloody Johnsons', and who, if all accounts are true, were fully entitled to it. I told of their great feastings and of their disappointments too, when one day they would all draw in their chairs and lift the cover off such a dish as this, and lo and behold, all that lay there was a polished set of spurs. The chairs would be scraped back and the men thunder off on their horses to bring back beef 'on the hoof' from 'over the Border', and apparently they didn't boggle at stealing a maiden at the same time and bringing her home across the saddle. This my old grandfather, assured me, kept the blood from getting 'sib'.

I didn't think much of my story-telling the next day, when again I reached for the dish, and uncovered a brace of cartridges, their brassy eyes winking at me! I, too, scraped my chair back, and returned later, tired, but triumphant, with a cock grouse and a blue hare.

Eight weeks old — we couldn't wait longer — the piglets scampered round the market ring in an endless chain, skins shining like silver sixpences, tails tightly curled, as if Dame Nature had laughingly signed them off with a merry doodle. Up they went. Four pounds, five, six, seven. Eleven times seven pounds!

"Yes, please, I'll take it in cash!"

The leather of my sporran crackled as I stuffed the notes in. Cakes and sweets for the children, a box of chocolates for Irralee. I felt like a millionaire and, light of step, set off for home.

2

The tops of the big peaks were soon covered in snow; the red deer had moved down below the white line; a robin skirled on the byre roof and, strung across the sky, skeins of wild geese traced the shadowy fingers of an icy hand that hovered over the land.

Round the fire of glowing birch logs, we planned to beat the winter and meet the year to come, and on the fireplace lay the stones that we had painstakingly gathered off our hill. I could see them fashioned into the shape of everything that was truly Highland, something that the summer visitors would beat a path to Croft Douglas to see and take home with them. My best ideas always came to roost in the early hours of the morning. I dug Irralee in the ribs at 3.00 am.

"Highland Cattle. That's it!"

She protested sleepily. One eye surveyed me anxiously for a moment, looking for a fever. Reassured, it again became a placid pool, and the curtain lowered. But in my mind I could see them — the stones of our destiny turning into Highland cattle, mounted with real horns. I couldn't wait for the morning.

With the dawn came reality. Difficulties, snags, frustration. Nothing would go right. I hurled the stones from me and felt better. I must have a model, but I couldn't find one for miles around, apart from one old cow which tossed a forelock back to assure me her granny was once chased by a Highland bull!

So it was Westering Ho! to the Pedigree Highland Cattle Sale at Oban and I had a feeling that, once again, our bank balance was going west too.

The stage was set. The auctioneer mounted the rostrum, blew twice into his microphone, rolled his eyes up to the big, impassive clock face as its hands pointed unwaveringly to zero hour. He smote the woodwork with his baton and tier upon tier of faces swivelled in his direction, belted earls rubbing shoulders with the drovers. The chattering ceased. Cigar smoke, spiralling lazily upwards took smooth, evasive action to avoid the intertwining of pipe and cigarette, but was, nevertheless, drawn into the overhanging classless haze.

"Ladies and gentlemen. Number One in the catalogue is 'Dossan Bhuidhe'."

As if he had said 'Open Sesame' the big, twin doors flew open to disgorge a beautiful Highland cow. A blue-blooded aristocrat with a pedigree in 'the Gaelic' as long as the yellow hair that flowed down her flank and on, in a cascade of burnished gold. She padded round with an effortless gait, little spurts of sawdust dancing round her feet. Round and round she went, shaggy head held high, proudly displaying a magnificent six foot span of horn. Her owner took his stance beneath the booming voice. Bids came mysteriously through the raised eyebrow, a wagging forefinger or nod of the head.

Yes, this could be our model, beautifully proportioned. I peered at her eyes — I knew nothing of the art of cattle buying, but this was important to me. Underneath the golden forelock I met a steady, honest gaze. The voice was halting now. Slow, cajoling, but not considering me.

"Going."

I jumped up and down, my throat too dry to commit the outrageous sin of shouting out. My catalogue beat the air like a windmill. That did it!

"Going, going, gone."

The baton descended. The bees of conversation buzzed again, some high and excited, but the Gaelic ones low and lilted. A white-coated attendant approached me and I whispered my identity. He marched back to the auctioneer who acknowledged me with a nod and 'I'll know you next time' smile.

"Sold to Croft Douglas."

A Cavern yawned open and she of the golden forelock was swallowed up. The sale went on, but I sat there in a trance. I owned a pedigree Highland cow. Through my trance the auctioneer's voice addressed the multitude.

"Quiet please, and keep those catalogues down. The next animal is just a little excited, that is all."

Muffled thumps and groans could be heard. We caught a glimpse of the attendant's flailing arms and legs as a tornado of horn and hair launched itself into the ring. Here was something that would blanche the countenance of a matador. The attendants wafted out of the ring, like leaves before a gale, as the animal charged round. The very air was charged too — with adrenal electricity!

Rearing on its hind legs, the cow made a near successful attempt to hurdle the high iron guard rails round the ring, and hung for a moment with brisket suspended on the top rail, hooves beating the air over the heads of the spectators. They cringed back in a wave that sent a ripple running through the crowd. The auctioneer's voice lashed the attendants with scorn.

"There's nothing to be afraid of."

In a courageous attempt to encourage this opinion the owner, over six feet of brawny Islander, warily sidled his sixteen stones into the ring and, muttering softly in Gaelic, reached his spot under the auctioneer. The Fury, cheated in her attempts to annihilate the attendants, spun round and spotting him was for a moment locked, eye to eye. The great horns lowered, twin blasts down the nostrils announced 'Steam Up'.

The big man's face twitched as his nerve drained away. Slowly, he backed against the woodwork when, behind him, a small panel opened and miraculously his bulk disappeared into the tiny cavity, like a rabbit down a pop hole. The rostrum shuddered under the impact of the direct charge and the auctioneer, now a bit shaken too, put an end to the Roman holiday by signalling for the exit to be opened.

Like a rocket the beast streaked for the opening and, with a final sweep of her horns, ably assisted the doorkeeper's climb over the rails as he cleared the top in full flight, momentarily displaying the neat rows of tackets in his boots. Thundering hooves drummed their way into the distance and normal business was resumed.

The animals came and went until 'Eurach Dearg' translated as the 'Red Lady' attracted me, and I looked with interest. She was every inch a lady, her gleaming Titian hair flowing like a silken gown.

"Guaranteed in calf," the auctioneer encouraged.

The bidding was surely ridiculously low and my forefinger, entirely of its own volition, wagged once, twice. Smack! Down went the hammer. No hesitation this time.

"Sold to Croft Douglas."

The thuds of my heart drowned the groaning bank book. One red, one yellow. My legs felt stronger now and I turned to go, but for one last fateful second I listened to that voice.

"Fraoch and her calf, surely a bargain."

The voice gripped me with a hoarse, enchanted whisper.

"Two for the price of one."

Dared I look? I did. There she was, a beautiful bunch of Gaelic heather with a teddy-bear calf following her mother's every move and sticking to that bronzed flank like a burr. I dreamily thought of the children's faces. The baton's crack awakened me.

"Sold to Croft Douglas."

My heart thumped anew, but this time the bank book didn't make a sound. I knew that it had died.

In the morning, yesterday's dream was a reality. The Highland cattle posed in all their glory on our own hill. The wind of their coming blew joyfully up the strath into the glens, and the silver birches, rustling with excitement, reached down and gently tickled the hairy backs.

3

Boats, like a lot of things, were a new experience for me at Croft Douglas. Our land swept down to meet the waters of Loch Tummel and, in doing so, earned us the right to fish the entire loch. Our first boat was a little plywood dinghy, whose many holes and patches were held together by a generous mixture of tar, paint and faith!

My education on the water was one of trial and error, until I learned to read the varying moods of the loch, the sky and the hills, and to appreciate just how quickly a scene could change from a peaceful calm to a turmoil of the elements. How a wind, with the devil shrieking in it, could blow in from the west, gather up the clouds through the hills of

Glencoe and throw them, chilled and grey, into the face of the sun. Then on, swiftly gaining strength to howl across the open Moor of Rannoch and, with a roar, strike the waters at the head of the loch, quickly whipping them into a team of wild white-maned 'horses', sending them galloping down the water at a furious rate. It is a frightening experience to be caught in the path of this stampeding horde, to feel the bosom of the waters heave with excitement as the pounding waves draw near.

It was like this on my first fishing trip when I set out alone to get some fish for the tea in my little cockle shell, and ventured into the middle of the loch. I had marked a spot, during the calm of the morning, where a fish had constantly agitated the water with a series of expanding circles. This was just about the place. Was the fish still at home? It was, and we were soon deeply engaged. A big one — it used nearly all my line to plumb the depths, but at last I was coaxing it nearer. A large dorsal fin neatly sliced the water and I knew my landing net would never hold it. Suddenly the bottom seemed to drop out of the boat as it curtsied deeply to a billowing wave. Coming up out of the curtsey, I gasped in horror at the mountainous rollers racing towards me. Quickly I wedged the rod, kicked off my wellington boots and grabbed the oars. With a crash of thunder the 'white horses' struck. For a second the boat stood up, pointing pathetically to the angry sky, then joined the racing steeds down the loch.

A curling wave reached me, choking me in a flying cloud of foaming spray, and viciously tearing an oar from my hand. I waited, wondering when I would join it in the water. But my frail little craft was still right way up and I could see a long arm of trees, their frenzied arms beckoning to me. Cautiously, I used my remaining oar to steer slightly towards them — not too much or I would have been rolled over like an apple barrel. The branches rushed to meet me and the 'horses', tired of their load, tossed the boat high in the air dropping it on the shingle with a sickening crunch. Leaping out, I pulled it clear of the clawing waves, my rod still

11

wedged in the stern. The line was tight too! I wiped the water from my eyes — my fish was still there! I guided it through the shallows, up, up on to the gurgling pebbles. What a monster! With a splash we engaged in an all-in wrestling match, rolling about together in a wild, flapping, watery embrace. Wriggling and twisting, the big fish slipped out of my clutching hands and through my arms.

I threw myself lengthwise to cut off its retreat to the deep. The sucking shingle shifted under me to join the backwash of the greedy waves, whose clammy fingers strove to regain us both. Feeling deeper water, the fish propelled itself forward in a last desperate effort. I plunged my arm under its huge sliding flanks and, with one gigantic heave, sent it flying through the air to fall on the lochside's grassy bank. Staggering after it I fell, too, hugging the sweet, fresh turf, sticking my fingers deep down into the good solid earth. The trout lay in front of me, bathed in a beauty of colour no artist could hope to emulate. As moments slipped past I knew that the golden bronzes, the shimmering silver, the tints of violet, red and blue were fading. Soon the glorious galaxy of colour would be gone for ever, and I was responsible.

I thought back to one day in that first hungry winter when the cupboard was more than bare. Irralee had spotted a cock pheasant on the hill behind the house and I carefully and successfully stalked it, with grim intent. The bead of my gun covered the bird fairly and squarely. My finger tightened on the trigger but the morning sun, peering over the hill tops, shot first, setting the delicately painted plumage aflame, presenting me with a blaze of brilliance I could not possibly extinguish. I crept back to the house mumbling,

"That bird was too quick for me."

But Irralee knew and wordlessly produced the last tin of beans. I can hear it still, the metallic 'clunk' as she set it sharply on the table, but I felt, too, her understanding and the beans didn't taste so bad after that.

I studied my fish again. It would provide, royally, for our hungry brood and I told myself, it must weigh at least eight and a half pounds. That would make it roughly twelve years old, more than a ripe age for any trout and I felt indignant over all the little trout it must have swallowed in that time. Standing up, I tied the boat to a tree. That mad career down the loch had taken me more than three miles along the shore, so I picked up the big fish and made for home.

My next trip to the loch convinced me that it was time I had a sturdier and more worthy craft. A neighbour, Angus, a character cast in the mould of a peat bog, moss and heather, had joined me on this occasion complete with rod, lures, flask, lots of enthusiasm and his favourite Cairn terrier, Sandy. We were soon launched and had left the world behind. My friend was seated at one end, myself at the other, whilst Sandy sniffed around the bottom. Our rods whipped to and fro, conducting the rhythmic flight of the artificial flies — a little jig on the surface, then whisked away to sing through the air and dance again, on what looked like a more promising spot.

"Come on, little trootie," my partner was crooning, then softly cursing in Gaelic when they heeded him not.

We were oblivious to everything, or almost everything, when I felt a sudden chill around my legs. Forcing my eyes from the lures, I looked down. Goodness, the boat was half-full of water.

"Dhia mo graidh."

That's the Gaelic again as my companion discovered our plight.

"Don't move."

The water had risen rapidly to the seats. For some unknown reason we were sinking. I looked wildly around and my eyes settled unbelievingly on Sandy, now perched high in the stern with an unholy grin on his face. Clutched tightly in his teeth was the whisky cork which, up to this moment, had done noble service as the bung! The boat was almost full, a sudden move would be fatal. I slipped a large handkerchief from my pocket and gently leant forward, plunging my arm down. My feverish fingers found the hole and effectively stuffed the hankie in. At the other end of the boat a baling can was now working steadily, the Gaelic profanity had a softer tone and, as it changed to an island courting song, I knew we had won.

But it was not until we had rowed gently to the shore that we relaxed. The terrier nipped nimbly ashore, still wearing that devilish grin. His little pink tongue slipped out past the whisky cork and lolled about drunkenly. At that we both collapsed and laughed and laughed, till our sides were aching and Sandy, releasing his trophy, cocked his head to one side and laughed too.

The big boat, a lifeboat from a drifter, duly arrived and Angus, who had procured it for me, organised the launching. This, I gathered, was to be a serious affair and carried out in the best traditions. Neill had his camera to record the occasion for prosperity. To his wife, who, I'm sure, had spent the night in sleepless repetition of her piece, had fallen the honour of bestowing the name. Hamish, a local 'mine host', was also there; small, dapper and efficient. He took up his stance and awaited, with professional aplomb, his part in the proceedings. Who could question the virginity of the neatly folded napkin, the stamp of silver on the tray, the quality of the amber liquid glowing warmly in the glasses, or the expertise with which the whole was balanced?

All hands were mustered around the delivering transport and the boat, resplendent in her new coat of paint, bowed her head to slide down the ramp. With a great deal of pushing, pulling and coaxing she started to move and eventually settled fair and square at the top of the wooden skids which ran down the steep bank to meet the water.

". . . and God bless all who sail in her," the voice rang with conviction. The tiny bottle of 'Babycham', which dangled from a rod stuck in the ground, was seized and propelled towards the boat. 'Clunk', the bottle hit the target but bounded back intact, and was fielded in a catch that would have done credit to any cricket match. Another swing, with all the fury of frustrated feminity behind it and 'Clunk'. Neill strode forward to back up his 'better half' and it was he who, this time, made the return catch.

There was a silence that you could slowly chew on, then Neill, having expanded his lungs to bursting point, threw back his arm, and with a roar that echoed the length and breadth of the valley, hurled the offending bottle to destruction. It made direct contact and smashed to atoms and Hamish, who was keeking enquiringly from the other side, got the entire contents, full in the face. The napkin served admirably for mopping up operations, and a dram all round soon restored equilibrium.

Angus and I seated ourselves in the boat, ready to conduct her maiden voyage, but as I raised my hand to give the signal for willing hands to push us off, I noticed Angus' face had changed colour. His mouth opened and shut soundlessly. Perhaps, I thought, some of the whisky had gone the wrong way, and was ready with sympathy for such a waste. But he was pointing now, pointing to a dark circle in the bottom of the boat. There was no bung in it!

Shaking off his apathy, Angus conjured up a thick wad of tow and thrust it into the gaping hole. Not a second too soon as the boat, swiftly gathering speed, charged down the skids like a thirst-crazed bull, and hit the water with a resounding smack. Angus, in the bow, got the full benefit of the upsurging wave, which lovingly enveloped him. Fortunately, the cheers drowned the wording of Angus' address to the water.

The 'Kelpie' was launched and under way.

4

The boats, when not in use, lay snugly side by side in the quiet backwater of our little bay. So they were until, one day, Irralee came rushing into my workshop full of excitement about the strange craft that were sailing up the loch. Indeed, on seeing them in the distance, I thought they must be ghosts of some long lost galleons which had sailed right out of time. I reached for the telescope and drew the fantastic shapes into the palm of my hand. There was something very familiar about their lines. Yes, I was sure now. They were our own boats, but complete with tall masts and fully rigged with multicoloured sails. I was dumbfounded and outraged. Rapidly through my head ran the tales of tough nomadic trampies who, in the past, had stolen lochside boats and, indeed, on one occasion when caught in the act, had manhandled and tossed the unfortunate owner into the loch! This, I was determined, would not be my fate and I paused only to lift my gun.

The run down the hill and through the lochside woods, with the sight of the empty boat bay, brought me nicely to boiling point. Like an Indian Scout I wriggled the last twenty yards where the undergrowth thinned out, and threaded my way along the rocks to a vantage point which reached out into the water. There I lay motionless. The small boat was coming towards me and I calculated that, on its present course, it would pass the point about fifty yards out. It drew almost opposite. I gasped when I saw how grossly overloaded and how dangerously low the little craft rode in the water, but marvelled at the speed she was making, and the masterly set of her sails. Five, six shapes I counted, and this in a craft designed for three.

Jumping up I bellowed "Come in", and waved again and again, my arm sweeping towards the bay in the most commanding gesture I could muster. For a moment the boat

16

seemed to falter then, with a haughty flirt of her stern, she indolently turned away, despisingly waving a pocket handkerchief sail, which ran up to pass the billowing mainsail, and opened out at the top of the mast to greatly assist her flight. In the face of this outrage I felt the icy calm of a mountain tarn run through me, and picking up my gun, took cool and deliberate aim at the top of that saucy sail. The crash of my shot reverberated across the water and echoed and re-echoed among the surrounding hills. The little boat rocked violently and confusion reigned aboard. I leapt to the top of the rocks, the wind tugging at the pleats of my kilt, a trail of smoking cordite curling wickedly from my gun.

"Will you come in now?" I roared, "Or share the next one among you?"

I marvelled at the cold menace of my words, and felt them absorbed by the opposition. A voice drifted across the lapping waters.

"Vee come."

Cloaked with a thick foreign accent, it hung about with the uncertainty of a stranger. This was something I hadn't expected, but as I tramped impatiently up and down the shingle I knew that, for the moment at least, I had the advantage.

As the overloaded boat wallowed into the bay I caught, and recognised the murmured gutteral exchange which faded to silence as, one by one, the Germans lined up before me. They were a formidable looking crew, young, athletic, all dressed alike in reefer jackets and leather shorts. My eyes narrowed down to the knives, lightly sleeping in their hide sheaths. I mustn't let this troop settle.

"Who is your leader?" I snapped.

Eyes consulted and only one pair had the light of understanding. The owner of these advanced one step.

"It is Babu," he said, "Out there", and with arm extended, he pointed at the big boat, which was now cautiously poking an inquiring nose towards us.

"Tell him", and I punctuated each word with a tap on the

gun barrel, "to come in."

With frantic gesticulations the message was translated through cupped hands and reluctantly the big boat heaved her bulk into the bay. I could count her crew now. Seven, eight, nine. Nine and six make fifteen. Things were adding up a bit! A lanky figure vaulted lightly over the side and padded towards me. I studied a face that gave nothing away.

"You are the leader, Babu?"

The German drew himself up to well over six feet.

"Yes."

Then, halting at each word,

"Vot do vee do now?"

His eyes treated me to a flinty gaze; long hands sat tensely on his hips, fingers splayed down, one set, unwittingly

18

perhaps, to cover the knife shaft. Now was the time to strike again and before you could say 'Sgian dhubh' I had whipped mine from my stocking.

"Do you know the penalty for boat and sheep stealing in the Highlands?"

With a hiss he replied, "No."

Slowly I drew the gleaming blade across my throat and jerked my head back in a horrible gesture. Babu's nostrils expanded like mushrooms on a moist morning. He stepped back.

"Nein, nein."

I followed up with an emphatic "Ja, ja," and watched his morale give a dying twitch in his cheek and drain slowly away to be absorbed by the sand at his feet.

Now, I thought, is the time to be magnanimous. I put my sgian dhubh back to bed in my stocking and leant on my gun.

"But, of course, I realise, now, that you are visitors to the Highlands and know nothing of our laws and customs."

The flood tide of relief brought a spate of colour back to Babu's face and I continued.

"Tell your men to dismantle the sails and I will inspect for damage."

He turned to bark the order and they rushed to obey.

Down came the masts (well-trimmed, tapering trees) and the sails were neatly rolled, sailor fashion. I pointed to the fractured oar. Babu frowned and it was seized by the 'bodies' for a quick and efficient splicing job. Everything else seemed to be in order. I finished at the stern of the boat and gave a tug at the anchor rope. It was broken. There was nothing at the end of it. Wheeling round, I whipped out,

"Where is the anchor?"

Babu spread two huge hands, palms upwards in a 'disclaim all knowledge' gesture.

"That boat was anchored to a new three point anchor," I said.

Babu, whose face had assumed a babe-like innocence asked,

"But where is it now?"

I slipped on the mailed glove again.

"When you took that boat the anchor was dragged with it. It is out there, somewhere." I pointed to the wide expanse of the loch.

"And," I added quietly and finally, "I want it back."

Babu wilted slightly and spun round.

"Hans!" he roared.

A handsome youth with a shock of blond hair leapt to Babu's bidding, stripped off his clothing and plunged into the water. He carved his way through the waves with practised ease and upending, seal fashion, disappeared, to surface further out, blowing like a porpoise. He dived again, and I wondered, idly, how he had achieved that tanned bottom. Each successive dive took Hans further and further out until his head assumed the size of a tennis ball.

I was just on the point of calling a halt to the proceedings knowing the treacherous undercurrents which could cramp the strongest swimmer, when Hans suddenly erupted with a cry that made the seagulls stop to listen, and an arm waving in triumph. Babu spat out the orders. Three more men stripped and, looping coils of rope round their gleaming bodies, raced for the water. The remainder formed a chain and advanced behind them. In a series of spectacular dives Hans and his helpers plumbed the depths to get the anchor. The rope was then joined to another and yet another until the main body had hold of it, and heaved mightily.

Two henchmen deposited it at my feet. This was Babu's moment. Like one who has just accomplished the impossible he bowed low and crooned,

"The anchor."

Everything was now ship-shape and we took leave of each other nonchalently.

I tried my best German.

"Auf wiedersehen."

The lanky German permitted his features the luxury of a delighted grin.

"Auf wiedersehen."

I felt this was the right ending for the episode. International relations remained unstrained and we parted in mutual respect. I turned to go but after a step or two, turned again.

"There is just one thing," I said, "I regret having to open fire. It seemed the only language you were prepared to understand."

Babu jacked himself down until his long, bony legs stuck out at right angles. Slowly, and with a wealth of meaning, he banged his knees together, once, twice, three times.

"Vee understood," he smiled.

5

We have no near or visible neighbour to east, west or north, but to the south, across the loch, a farmhouse sits on the hillside and gives us the comfort of human companionship. We hear the raucous cackle of geese, the barking of the sheepdogs and, on occasions, the house cow bawling when her calf is sold.

When darkness fell the yellow lamplight chummily winked at us and reached out like the warm grasp of a friendly hand, banishing all the shadows of loneliness.

"Who will be to bed first?"

The golden glow is extinguished.

"Oh, they've beaten us tonight, just when we were thinking of calling it a day."

Or, perhaps we are cosily tucked up in bed and have a last peep out of the window. The light still beams across the water. We pull the blankets up to our chins and exult.

"Got you this time, stop-ups!", or not so smugly, "Do you think they are having a ceilidh?"

In the winter mornings we jockey to win the early rising

race with varying fortunes.

But one night the neighbour's light gleamed with a new polished brilliance and boastfully blazed over the loch. They had acquired 'the electricity' and we rejoiced with them, but felt a stab of envy as the tang of paraffin still followed us around.

Electricity where it is made, right here in the Highland lochs, was at a premium and we watched the high voltage lines pour the stuff south. But for us it meant the installation of a transformer to tap the main line and, as there were no near neighbours, we would have to bear the cost alone.

We were quoted a price that made our hair stand on end! Later, we were given the opportunity of paying an outsize electricity bill in the form of a guaranteed figure over a period of seven years. For nights we totted up figures of estimated expenditure on oil, fuel and everything that goes to provide light and heat. It was a big gamble, but I was all for it. The power alone would save us countless hours of labour.

The men arrived to fix the transformer and set up the poles. Beneath a few inches of soil on the hill there is solid rock, but they were determined men with sticks of dynamite. Soon explosions rocked the glen and at various intervals soil, rock chips and boulders flew high in the air. All went well until the supply of detonators ran out. A short delay while more were obtained then the blasting resumed to herald the day when a big switch at the power station would be thrown up and we would have the satisfaction of knowing that an awful lot of people were doing without electricity until our line was connected.

Angus was there on the big day with his double-barrelled shotgun and the inevitable bottle. The gun roared, the switches were snapped down and the lights blazed on. Angus made a speech and solemnly presented us with a dozen candles for "the power cut, when it comes." And the bottle went round. The neighbours switched on their congratulations and we beamed across at one another. We were on level terms again.

After many long years of filling lamps and chopping wood we will never fail to appreciate or take for granted the sheer luxury of producing light and heat with the flick of a finger. But the best feeling of all is to turn the 'Queen's View' corner on a dark night and see, over two miles away, the bright eye that watches, waits and warmly welcomes your home-coming.

Whilst the electric wires sneak surreptitiously through the hills, there are other wires threading their way along the Strathtummel road; long, thin, sometimes vital lines of communication. In our isolation we faced all kinds of situations and coped as best we could with the emergencies that arose from time to time.

But there came a day when we decided that we had struggled too long without the swift direct aid of the telephone and the time had come to apply for installation. It wasn't as easy as that. We were placed on the waiting list and told that it might take up to two years to connect us! Two years, it seemed an eternity! But out of the blue came a request for permission to place a pole on our land to strengthen the existing telegraph line. I quickly gave my blessing to the project on the condition that our telephone was installed at the same time. This seemed to me a simple 'tit for tat' agreement. It was not the view of officialdom and the cars started to call and each successive vehicle grew in size with the status of the individual, but I stuck to my point. If the pole went up I never noticed it, but the telephone people kept their part of the bargain and the instrument was installed without further delay.

It sat there, a block of bakelite with a bland expression, always on duty, ready to speak or be spoken to. It was there to summon the doctor when his services were required, there for assurance when delay was causing anxiety. It called out the 'Breakdown' for stranded motorists and once procured a pair of trousers (there being *no* such article at Croft Douglas) for a too-enthusiastic photographer who had ventured to take a close-up of the Highland cow Kirsty and her new-born calf.

Kirsty was of our breeding who, as a calf, had become very tame and was thoroughly petted and spoiled by all and sundry. Familiarity does indeed breed contempt and Kirsty, grown up now with a baby of her own, feared no man. This foolish photographer drew up in his smart sports car and, probably to impress the charming damsel at his side, dived through the fence and marched straight up to Kirsty. In doing so the young man placed himself between the Highlander and her calf (a position no cattleman would ever get himself into, certainly if he knew Kirsty), but I was never given the chance to explain this to him.

Kirsty, eyes blazing with affront, gathered herself and charged. The young man almost won the race to the fence, but Kirsty was there in the final stride and tossed him over the

wire. The top strand was heavily barbed and the young man rolled down the bank, considerably shaken but unhurt. On the wire hung the best half of his trousers, on Kirsty's horns hung the camera, and the young man hung his head!

It is when the storms sweep the hills that the telephone assumes an importance all its own. Our eldest children had graduated from the little school at Strathtummel and daily travelled the long twisting miles to Pitlochry by bus. One morning, not long after they had gone, a snowstorm blew out of the east with unexpected ferocity. We frowned back at the angry sky; two hours of solid snowing and not a sign of letting up. By 'phone we contacted the school with word that the outlying conditions were getting bad. Yes, they were worried, too. The children would be sent home right away. We checked the clock, they should be here within the hour. But the hands of time travelled past the alloted span. Outside, the snow rose higher and swept across the road in sweeping drifts. The 'phone rang with agitated insistence — word had been received in Pitlochry that the school bus was stuck in the Killiecrankie Pass, a point about six miles from us.

What to do now? We rang in various directions. Had anyone seen the snowplough? Not a sign. We could do no more in the meantime. The clock described another circle, then began again. We waited and watched. Once again the 'phone rang, making us jump as its demanding clamour broke the waiting silence. The snowplough had been spotted up the Great North Road, had been given the message and was now heading towards the Pass.

Another circle round the clock, but tension had eased a bit when, round the bend, headlights stabbed the darkness, outlining the myriads of snowflakes. Then, gouging its way through the drifts, tossing the snow aside with a growling roar, came the snowplough and, crawling in its wake like a faithful St. Bernard dog, was the school bus. How good it felt to have everyone under the roof and, as the children tucked into bowls of hot soup, the telephone sat, with shoulders squared, after a job well done.

25

6

Chance, with a flick of her fickle finger, brought Tarra to Croft Douglas. Born on the south side of Loch Tummel, this beautiful, black and white collie bitch belonged to a sheep farmer, and there was nothing about working blackface sheep that she didn't know.

She then had two loves — to work and to eat. I don't know which was the stronger, but she threw herself into both occupations with all the energy life could muster. The peaks held no terror for her, she could leap the rocks and corries along with the mountain goats and skim the heather like a greyhound, covering countless miles to gather together, and bring in, the sheep. The wildest 'blackie' that was ever lambed never got away from Tarra.

In her idle moments the insatiable appetite took command. Anything from the skin of a rabbit to an unburied, decaying sheep, was grist to her mill; the bones of a mountain hare, the carcase of a grouse, and how well she looked on it! Her long hair shone like the raven's wing, her brown eyes deep with understanding, overlooked a black nose, moist with the freshness of the morning dew. The gloss of her coat was largely due to her passion for eggs. She could clean a grouse nest quick as a wink, and, if her luck were out in the heather, or the nesting season over, she would slip unobtrusively into the nearest henhouse.

Indeed, on one occasion she was seen nosing under a broody hen and, as the stupid bird crooned contentedly, was deftly robbed of her clutch of eggs.

Tarra knew how to relax too and, when not working or eating, no time was ever spent in unnecessary standing around. She flopped down with every fibre and muscle turned to jelly, making a flagstone look like a feather bed.

One night, when she was still with the sheep farmer, and at the one and only time that another urge took precedence over work and food, Tarra diligently ate her way out of her kennel and slipped away with some non-descript mongrel for a little illicit love-making. The carefully laid plans for her breeding were whisked away with the chaff and the thistle down, while her chosen husband, with trial record and impeccable family tree, waited in vain!

The pups were duly born and the shepherd presented the motley crew for the farmer's inspection. The verdict was short and to the point.

"Leave her something to take the milk off."

But here there was a misunderstanding, and the complete litter was despatched. If Tarra felt like mourning she was never given the opportunity.

This was the time of the big sheep gatherings, and every dog was required to sweep the hills from dawn to dusk. But it was too much for Tarra, the milk was heavy, hot and hard upon her and, time after time, she threw herself into the chilling waters of the hill burns to cool the fever in her body. She ran and ran until the dancing fleeces bobbed elusively ahead and, exhausted, she fell, unable to rise again.

It was shortly after this that I chanced to meet the farmer and asked him if he had a dog that would do for working the cattle. I had learned by this time that the hill sheepdog's working life is a comparatively short one and, when muscles tire and joints stiffen, and a lolling tongue constantly flies the distress signal, it is time to give the dog an easier task. Herding cattle is usually the answer; a job requiring all the old skill, but without constant exertion.

I know that when this moment arrives every farmer, worth his salt, remembers the devotion and labours of the past, and sees to it that the animal is happily placed.

So I was led round to Tarra's kennel. She looked up at me with a kindly look, and the straw of her bed danced to the thump of her tail. The farmer was shaking his head.

"A good dog spoiled by a stupid mistake, but if you look well after her and she gets back the use of her legs, you won't get a better dog."

Tarra tried to get up and move towards us but tumbled forward helplessly. I gathered her up in my arms and took her home in the car.

After a fortnight, with care and affection, Tarra was on her feet again, smiling as only she could. With lips curled tightly back over flashing white teeth, she made herself sneeze and sneeze! We found out that this smile was produced only on two occasions, either when she was very pleased or trying to cover up some misdeed.

Highland cattle do not take kindly to dogs, so I had to introduce Tarra as gently as possible. She quickly learned the drill, to coax rather than drive, moving the herd softly but firmly, and became invaluable for, quickly and quietly, moving the animals from place to place. She soon got to know all the 'breakaway' points between pastures and, with split second timing, would be there to stop a gap with 'No road this way' written all over her face, just as the leading cow reached it.

Fraoch, the cow with the heathery name and temperament to match, was the only one to challenge the collie's authority. One day she caught Tarra in an unguarded moment and with a lightning, scythe-like sweep of her horns, she tossed the collie high in the air. Fortunately the turf was springy and yielded to soften Tarra's fall. She jumped to her feet, shaken and apprehensive. Fraoch went quickly into the attack again and Tarra backed away.

This would never do. I flashed the 'Go in' signal and the collie, without question, moved lionheartedly into the duel. Weaving an elusive pattern she sidestepped the slashing horns and dodged the flailing hooves. With a quick, encircling movement as the hairy tasselled tail sailed past her nose, she seized the huge bell-like tuft and held on grimly.

Round and round the cow spun in a vain attempt to reach her adversary and Tarra sailed through the air like some death-defying aerial artist. The cow suddenly tired and turned to join the herd and only then was the vice-like grip on the tail released, and Tara trotted serenely behind her, turning once to show me her smile.

Anything, from a curl of apple peel to a chunk of cowhorn was food to Tarra. She knew to visit the workshop when the horns were being fitted to the model cattle and would wait expectantly until the chips of horn flew around. Then she would chump away at them and, when her jaws tired, suck appreciatively, as though each fragment were a lamb chop fresh from the grill.

Tarra's ambitions grew with her taste for horn. One day I caught her sneaking past the workshop door, dragging a full set of antlers. I left her in no doubt as to the view I took of her latest idea in tasty snacks.

Early one morning I was walking past a croft on the hill and stopped to have a word with the lady of the house, who was selecting a peat from the stack. I failed to notice Tarra, who had been at my heel, glide silently through the open doorway. But soon the peace of the morning was shattered by an angry roar and, in the doorway, danced an irate giant in his shirt tails.

"A hairy divil has stolen my breakfast".

I looked down and there was Tarra, once more at my heel, licking her lips and smiling uncertainly. It transpired that the good man had just had his bacon and egg delivered to his bedside and was sleepily inhaling the succulent odours, when a black be-whiskered snout had cleaned the platter before his half-open eyes.

I apologised profusely, but the good lady would have none of it and, turning on the poor, breakfastless, shirt-tailed wretch berated him for being a no-good lie-a-bed. Tarra and I melted silently away and the tirade, like the bagpipes, sounded better from a distance.

There was the time when we thought Tarra was smitten with an attack of rabies, but a sample of the white froth from her muzzle proved to be whipped cream which had adorned a peach melba that Irralee had hidden away as a surprise.

Only once did I take Tarra shopping with me in Pitlochry. She got ahead of me in our dash from shop to shop and I bumped into her as she left the fishmonger's, her jaws folded over the edge of a wad of kippers. A sad tear slipped from one eye, but I couldn't be sure if it were the dew of contrition or due to the salty tang of the kippers. She was immediately banished to the back seat of the car, whilst I completed the purchases.

Always in a hurry, I got back into the car again and, absent-mindedly slung a two pound package of steak over my shoulder and drove off. Tarra must have thought this was a peace offering to signify all was forgiven. Not even a scrap of brown paper was left when I got home.

But it was at gathering up the sheep that Tarra was best and although we had none of our own — all our grazing was needed for the cattle — we had plenty of visitations from marauding sheep. Bands of 'blackfaces', especially in the hungry winter months, were attracted like nails to a magnet, to pastures untainted by their own kind. They would force their way through the march fences and leap the boundary walls, to plunder the precious grass and heather that had survived the elements.

Tarra defended us nobly against these rovers and would quickly return them to their own ground.

I remember the first occasion on which we met up with some of the trespassers; three blackface ewes, leaping like deer, had crossed the drystane dyke which forms our boundary to the east. Tarra looked up at me sharply and her eyes said,

"Did you see that?"

With a wave of my arm I sent the collie away. The sheep stamped their feet and danced nervously, but Tarra had also seen, or heard, something else. She ran wide of the sheep, cleared the boundary dyke like a swallow and disappeared. Within minutes the skyline bobbed about as hundreds of heads appeared and Tarra drove the entire neighbouring flock towards me. She evidently thought I had wanted sheep and was determined that she would show me what could be done about it! However, in time we understood each other, and an inclination of the head, or the wave of the hand, spoke volumes.

We had precious little time for play at Croft Douglas, but on these rare occasions Tarra loved to join in the fun and would romp with us like a puppy. I think she most enjoyed the swimming expeditions in the summer, when we all ran helter-skelter down the hill to the little bay to plunge and splash about in its cool waters.

Tarra joined enthusiastically in the swimming lessons, and quickly learnt a life-saving drill, which was one of the things she really took seriously. I would swim out for about thirty yards, throw my hand in the air and, with a wild splashing, simulate a fine state of panic.

Tarra, watching from the shore, would wait for my act to begin, her head cocked on one side, ears pricked, every hair bristling and every wriggle suggesting that the very sand underneath her was warming to white heat. At the first splash of distress she would hurl herself into the water and, summoning an amazing turn of speed, streak like a torpedo for her target. Her black nose would surge towards me, almost touching mine and her eyes, pools of responsibility, said,

"Now, you know what to do," and, in a swirling semi-circle, she presented her bushy tail for a tow. As I grasped it she would put on all steam and paddle determinedly for the shore.

When the children's swimming became more proficient their highlight was to be 'life-saved' by Tarra.

7

One day a speeding car left, in the dust of its retreat, the inert form of Tarra, our loved collie.

Oh! Those madly churning wheels which seek not the tempo of the highland roads, but claw them under at the fastest possible pace, leaving behind a devastating trail of destruction. The tiny wind-blown bunch of feathers that had delighted us this morning with its carefree song; the tattered, dusty, blood-bespattered piece of russet fur was the bright-eyed squirrel who had suddenly remembered just where he had hidden that last store of nuts who in his dash across the road — had never reached it; the spotted song-thrush, who had left the nest in a swift forage for food; Time really mattered to her, but now the bonnie blue eggs wait — and grow cold.

Gently we carried Tarra to the byre. The fresh, golden straw yielded comfortingly to the limp body. She didn't move, the brown eyes were open, but glazed and unseeing. Desperately, our fingers fluttered over her body and down her legs. Nothing seemed to be broken. No blood at the muzzle and the silky, white chest which had given her the Gaelic name, Tarraigheal, was unstained. It must be her back. As I touched it a brown eye awakened with the wild light of pain.

One of Irralee's tears splashed warmly on the back of my hand, saturating me with misery. What should I do?

I thought of my gun, resting coldly, aloof and unconcerned in its corner. It would be quick and merciful. But first, I must get another opinion. The telephone. I heard my voice wander over the lines like the inebriate who still wishes to remain a gentleman, stilted and correct. I gave the veterinary surgeon at Pitlochry all the details. What would be his verdict?

"Give her aspirins and twenty-four hours".

Relief poured over me, the evil moment had been postponed for at least two rounds of the clock.

We poured the aspirin, dissolved in warm milk, into the velvety pouch of Tarra's muzzle, and the resulting swallow was her first movement. The hours of the clock slowly wiped away the hours of vigil. Another new day and the cocks were crowing. Tarra moved her head once during the night, but that was all. She seemed quite peaceful, and we felt sure our regular doping had kept suffering to a minimum.

We had to leave her now for a while. There was milking to be done, stock to be fed and our own little brood to be got ready for school. Once this was all accomplished we found time for a quick breakfast and returned to Tarra.

Her 'borrowed' time was beginning to run out. I spoke her name softly and urgently "Tarra" The snowy white tip of her tail moved slightly: once, twice. I knelt down to say 'good dog', but could not find my voice.

In the afternoon the vet, who was passing, called in.

"Hmm. I think she still has a chance. Reminds me of a dog I once attended, hit by a train. Keep her absolutely quiet and give her another ten days".

Then, in tones coolly professional,

"Of course, you understand you will have to be prepared to put her down before, or at the end of, that time".

This brought me right down to earth again, and I found myself nodding a grave assent.

On the fourth day Tarra found the use of her forelegs. On the fifth she dragged herself two or three yards to the corner of the byre. I tried to discourage this by lifting her back to her bed and bidding her to 'lie still'.

Next day she had repeated the performance and we found her sticking her snout deep down into the straw, snuffing and sniffing excitedly. This time we let her be and the black muzzle soon emerged, triumphantly dragging out a piece of rabbit, a relic which the cat must have buried there against future food emergencies. It was far from fresh, but that mattered not one whit. She drooled over it as though it were the most succulent joint, and we hadn't the heart to take it from her. We felt, too, that this was indeed the old Tarra, and with such a spirit she must surely win her battle.

On the twelfth day (we gave her two extra for luck) when we opened the byre door, Tarra looked up expectantly as she had been outrageously spoiled with every kind of titbit. But this time we did not enter. I whistled, two ears sprang to attention, then called ner name. She propped herself up on her forelegs and, having achieved this, looked appealingly in our direction. I avoided her gaze and took a step away, saying,

"Come on, then".

With a low "Please wait for me" whine she gamely struggled to her feet.

Irralee and I hugged each other with delight. Tarra was actually standing on all fours! What did it matter if she could never again clear the dykes and gates with the easy grace of a flying swallow, or that we should never again witness the electrifying burst of speed that fairly scorched the heather tips?

Tarra was on her feet again and, as one who has drunk too deeply of the 'uisgebeatha' she wove an unsteady path towards us, leaving uncertainty and unhappiness to forage elsewhere.

8

Before the first light of dawn, before the cock rose to crow, I would waken and start to plan how to cram some of the multitudes of things to be done, into a new day.

The bracken and birch trees, that were choking the life out of the grass and heather on the hills, would have to be dealt with. There were cattle catching pens to be erected, fencing to be done, crops to be planned, repairs to the outbuildings and to the house itself.

I groaned as the list grew longer and longer and was tempted to succumb to the whispering, intimate warmth of the bed and drift off again on a trouble-free slumber cloud. It was then that I felt the weight of the millstone around my neck. My heart chilled, but not with the cold floor that my feet encountered.

It was still too dark to do anything outside, but I could get on with the modelling. I no longer threw things about and the Highland cattle pieces were, I thought, quite a success, thanks a lot to the beasts themselves, which had accepted me without question, and proved ideal subjects.

I had also made Red Deer stags, resplendently topped with antlers of hand-cut horn and shaped to give their 'tines' a 'Royal' count, the hinds were there too, with their light-hearted fawns.

I had tackled the blackface ewe and her lamb. These were modelled from the sheep on our neighbour's hill, and I also spent three alarming days in the pen of a blackface ram, who boasted a long pedigree, a heavy price tag, and a most fearsome pair of curling horns, which he kept constantly lowered and poised in my direction, until I really understood the full meaning of 'battering ram'.

The persistent thought which came to me was that if this keyed-up dynamo were to unwind, I would never have time to take evasive action, and would end up as a nasty mark on the whitewashed wall of the pen. But the Volcano never erupted, and his replica appeared under my hands.

Irralee became most proficient in putting on colour where it was needed and adding finishing touches, and so our first display of Croft Douglas handcrafts was ready.

We erected a little glass showcase near the roadside at the front of the house and, with infinite care, placed the Highland cattle on the first shelf, the family of blackface sheep on the middle, and a royal stag, with his hind and fawn, on the top. We shut the door, turned the key and walked self consciously back to the house; but outside, the little showcase waited, bold as brass.

'Tap, tap'. The thistle door-knocker beat on our hearts and announced our first customers, a charming couple who acknowledged our welcome with smiling faces, but understood not a word we said!

"Enchantant!" Ah, that was familiar, French. With gesticulation and mime in abundance we made our first sale.

"Au revoir." I managed that, but this must not happen again.

We dug out a French dictionary and swotted furiously. Our next customers were German! Fortunately, they had quite a bit of English and, as I had once volunteered for German lessons to escape 'fatigues' during R.A.F. training, things worked out very well on this occasion.

When the next Frenchman turned up I immediately threw myself into my piece.

"Ils sont fait de la pierre de la montagne". A glowing face swung its full beam on me and I was engulfed in a torrent of French, to which I had no answer.

In the course of time we have been visited by people from all over the world but, in the main, the bulk of our customers came from over the border, from England. For them, I also made models of tartanned clansmen doing battle with redcoats. But the Sassenachs ignored their own, and the poor redcoats remained without their assailants! So I concentrated on the kilted Highlanders.

I made one large model of a Chieftain in full regalia and, in a moment of enthusiasm, I had the idea of mounting this chieftain on a slab of granite and putting him on top of the showcase where the blade of his claymore would really catch the glint of the sun, and his eagle plume stir in the breeze. Surely, he would be really appreciated there.

He was. Within an hour, a fast car swooped on the case, and raced away, taking with it the result of long, long hours of work.

Gradually we expanded. A bigger showcase first, then we converted our largest room into a showroom, and here our handcrafts were exhibited, surrounded by everything that is Highland, which we had gathered together to keep our modelling on the correct lines. The royal stag held his head high and made light of that colossal spread of antler, higher up a golden eagle displayed its majesty and eight foot six spread of wing.

In an alcove, the blackcock fanned out the beautiful black and white fork of his tail and courted his mate, the grey hen. The blackcock's tail is worn by pipers and those who have a perfect specimen prize it and look after it carefully. They know it will be hard to replace. The blackcock is nobody's fool and as wild as the heather itself.

Here are the red grouse, the plumes of the cock bird warmly glowing with the wealth of good mahogany and there, the ptarmigan, snowy white in winter plumage and always looking just a little bit lonely, as anything must be that chooses to live on top of a mountain.

This was the atmosphere that I would have revelled in as a boy and, as I breathed it, I refused to grow up. Whenever I saw a youngster finger the wild cat skin or gaze, entranced, at the regal pose of the cock capercailzie, I knew exactly how he felt, and loved to tell him the stories behind the subjects.

One gentleman said he was bringing his boys up this way and asked if I would be good enough to tell them about the birds and animals of these parts. I readily agreed, but was more than surprised when he turned up one weekend in uniform, leading a complete troop of scouts, who advanced in waves upon the croft.

Soon I was submerged in a sea of neckerchieves, and woggles bobbed excitedly on all sides. I needed air and elbow room and was about to suggest that we climb Creag Mhor, where I would point out the ravens' nest and the eagles' eyrie, when one of those rare flashes of inspiration short-circuited my wandering thoughts.

For weeks I had been puzzling how to effect a repair on the big boat; a sharp stone had partially ripped off the iron which protected the wood of her keel, and I had no means of lifting the heavy vessel to replace it. Here was the answer.

Providence had provided man, or should I say, boy-power in abundance. I spoke of the birds on the lochside, the oystercatchers, greenshanks, widgeon, mallard and of their nests, too. I knew where they were. I knew, too, where every step had to be taken with careful thought, or we would tread on a clutch of gulls' eggs.

The Pied Piper never had a more enthusiastic following and I led them, a gay, excited throng, to the lochside. There I showed them the birds, the nests and the eggs and, having survived the bombardment of questions, I led them to the boat.

Would they like a sail to the islands, sanctuaries of the birds, and perhaps see a cormorant fishing?

How they would! But first, I explained, there was a small job of work to be done. Who are the strong ones?

Bodies thrust themselves forward, sleeves were jerked up to display an array of throbbing, bulging biceps. I ranged them shoulder to shoulder, fifteen to a side.

Hup! the big boat rose effortlessly in the air like a toy balloon, and remained there in awe-inspiring suspension. I slipped under and quickly screwed home the errant keel iron.

In obedience to my 'Slowly down now,' the heavy boat came down like a feather, and settled on the shingle with scarcely a sigh. Oh, that all my problems could have such an easy solution.

'A promise made is a debt unpaid', so we launched the boat and headed for the smallest island, a favourite breeding haunt of the Black-headed gull and Oystercatcher. As we glided quietly to its shores I pointed out the water hen's nest, a wave and waterproof raft, magically moored to a bunch of rushes by skilfully tied tendrils that allow for the unpredictable rise and fall of the water, and ensure the safety of their six brown speckled eggs.

On the island itself the boys were thrilled as they wove in and out of the pattern of gulls' nests, eggs, young gulls and chicks just newly hatched. But there in the centre, sitting on a cloud of snow white down, plucked from her own breast, sat the Queen of the island, the shy Canada goose. But this was as far as we went. With outstretched wings and hissing like a steam engine her mate suddenly appeared and, with steadfast advancing steps, shepherded us back to the boat, bidding us a brusque farewell and a final oath in goose language.

As our business increased, so the little showcase grew in size and when, one day a lean and tanned figure put his head round the door and announced in a friendly, casual drawl that he was from New Zealand, and that his nextdoor neighbour had told him he must be sure to call at Croft Douglas, I felt we were really getting somewhere.

There was the inoffensive little man who, I felt, had been relentlessly steered through life by his large, domineering partner and, as the tug follows the liner, he set his course around the showroom, but came to a sudden stop opposite the Highland bull model. And there he stayed, his head drooping lower and lower until he and the bull breathed into each other's nostrils.

The siren blasted the silence. "We'd better be going now."

The little man was shaken into wakefulness.

"I would like that bull."

His wife gazed at him in shocked surprise,

"Nonsense," she said, "I have just got something for you."

"But, but it's the bull I want." In desperation he fumbled for words like jittery fingers. The handbag gathered itself, snapped together with metallic finality and she sailed out of the door. In her wake staggered the little man pleading as if for his very life, and he, too, disappeared, leaving the echo of a strangled sob.

I would have given anything to have dashed after him and pressed the bull into his hands, but I knew this wasn't the way and that the little man must win or lose this battle by himself.

Next day the man walked steadily into the showroom and, funnily enough, no longer appeared to be little. Behind him, was a rather tired lady, who didn't look on the large side at all. She point wearily towards the Highland bull.

"Was that the one?"

The man bent down and his eyes gleamed as he breathed the fire from its nostrils.

"Yes, this is the one."

The visiting foreigners, in their varieties of colour, dress and creed, have, I think, one thing in common — their manners are impeccable. So it was with the swarthy, bearded figure who blew in with the hot, dusty winds of the desert still lurking in the folds of his garment saluted with a solemn, intricate wave of the hand, which ended by flicking the tail of his voluminous wrap over the left shoulder. He padded softly and silently around.

Now, I thought, if I had been a Crusader this fellow would probably be a member of the opposition, and I imagined myself in a deadly struggle on burning sands. But I was quite wrong. This son of the desert passed by the Claymore on the wall, ignored the glinting sgian dhubh, the cattle and staghorn knives, he never noticed the Highland warriors that had accounted for so many hours of hard work!

For him there was only one object in the showroom — a long, sturdy cromach, and, with burning eyes, he stood before it. A lean, brown finger slowly traced its way around the carved horn head and down, down its five feet of rich hazel shank.

I told him that this was a hill shepherd's stick, the head fashioned from the curling horn of a blackfaced ram and the shank, straight and true, a silver-hued hazel, cut from our own trees. See the gap in the horn head. It must take the span of four fingers to ensure it will catch the errant sheep safely, securely and comfortably round the neck.

He was intrigued by it, and I had a feeling that this man would be a shepherd himself, but I did not connect him with sheep. In the brown pool of his eye I saw him catching up the dusky straggler from his mission flock with a Highland cromach! He did not have to tell me he was going to take it. With slight embarrassment, he shifted a sandalled foot.

"I wish to pay," he said in perfect English, "but my money is worn next to the skin."

I laughed lightly and joked, "Then I suppose you will have to skin out for it then." And he did!

The base of his ribs, like the jaw of some monster, yawned over the silken belt encircling them, and there, sitting safely and snugly in his midriff, nestled a little purse. It disgorged a note, swallowed the change and disappeared in a billowing cloud of cotton.

Then there was the German girl with features cast in the outdoor mould. What fun the winds must have had running their tangling, tousling fingers through the blonde hair, and how they must have sighed on parting with such company. What did she want? Her mind was definitely made up before crossing the threshold. She wanted a ghillie's bonnet, not a new one, but a bonnet that had travelled the hills and gathered the mildew of many seasons, one impregnated with bog myrtle and heather, bleached and beaten by the sun and rain, mature with the malt of old whisky. Could I possible get her one?

I said I would do my best and her address was noted. I made lots of enquiries, but all the owners of eligible head gear refused to be parted from them, and looked too disgustingly healthy, showing no signs or inclination to depart for the Happy Hunting Ground. I tried to unnerve the older members of the fraternity by carelessly shrugging my shoulders and hinting grimly, "I can wait."

But they in turn, just smiled serenely, and I knew then that Highland ghillies never die. They just melt into the heather one day, bonnets and all!

I shelved the matter and hoped that the fraulein would forget as quickly as I hoped to. But a letter came, and with it a passionate appeal. This lassie had only one thing in her head, the bonnet.

I couldn't let her down, so I purchased a brand new one and buried it, without ceremony, in the nearest peat bog. I thought that after a suitable spell there I would use it to scare the crows off the corn. After that I was sure the elements would have added the required patina of mildew and I would add the final touch by piercing its weave with the barbed hook of a giant salmon fly, a hand-tied 'thunder and lightning.' Its brilliant colours would, I hope, add years to the bonnet.

I am sure that if the fraulein reads this she will forgive me. And I am sure, too, that after its sojourn in the bog the bonnet will carry the tang of good highland heather until the end of time.

I will remember, always, the day when a large party trooped into the showroom. All in their early twenties they were a cheerful crowd and, in turn, I was treated to a dazzling smile from a pretty, summer dress or a friendly nod or grin from blazer and flannels.

The room was filled to overflowing with a happy, excited atmosphere. The air was vibrant with feeling, yet everything was so strangely quiet, and the only voice I heard was my own. Then, suddenly, it came to me.

All those nice young people could neither speak nor hear and, as I watched, I realised that to them it did not matter. Their lips and gestures soundlessly framed all their conversations. Here was handicap turned to advantage, here was the priceless gift of silent expression, a people who were truly alive.

With an enquiring look a young man handed me a staghorn whistle. I showed him how it was made from the antler of a big stag and demonstrated, by blowing a clear piping note, how the shepherds and ghillies used its highpitched vibratory tone to signal to the dogs when working on the hill. I watched the sparkling blue eyes fan to a blaze of delight. He had heard it! His hand took the whistle from mine.

By this time I was feeling very much the odd man out, but from years of practice I had mastered the many soundless gestures, so I experimented and answered their questions equally soundlessly, sketching every word with my lips, adding in gesture a bit of colour and detail. It was my turn to be delighted. They understood me! The gulf closed, and with the intimacy of old friends, we shook hands and parted.

There was the little almond-eyed blossom who selected a framed photograph of myself embracing a Highland heifer, asked me to sign it, and tucked it away amidst the flowers of her kimono, saying,

"I will put th-ee-se on my cab-ee-nette in Hong Kong".

"But", protested the missionary who was escorting her party, "he is married and with children".

The jet black hair, swept up to match the butterflies' wings which adorned it, was unruffled.

"No mattel", she said.

The Indian ladies in their saris! How regally they moved and how alike they were. I remember seeing one with a small red circle on the centre of her forehead. It seemed to have been etched in lipstick. Was it a caste mark or pure decoration?

And the hostellers, in tackety boots, shorts and shirts, with their gigantic trappings, arrived and threw down their loads with deep sighs of relief, to don them again with many a strangled moan. I am sure these hardy young people endure all this, just for the sheer joy of dumping down their burdens.

I was watching an American prowling round the cream and chrome of a glinting Mercedes. He looked to me like a homesick lion which, returning to the safety and security of

its cage, finds his sanctuary locked up! Indeed, it proved to be
so, as the gentleman, driven to the limit of frustration, took
off his tiny Tyrolean hat, dashed it on the ground and jumped
on it, with a venom that poisoned the atmosphere.
Dramatically he addressed the Universe in general, in tones
shaking with emotion,

"We can split the atom, we can rocket into space, we can span the universe with satellites, but who the hell" and he grimly looked around him, "can get into my car?"

Intrigued, I examined the car and tried all the doors. Yes, he spoke truly. Short of breaking one of those tightly closed windows, how was anyone going to get into that car? The keys winked brightly from the dashboard, obviously enjoying an undisturbed and intimate embrace with the ignition.

I tried to lever open the windows with my sgian dhubh, but they lay tightly and snugly in their rubber beds. Idly, I ran the blade down the ventilation panel of the driver's window, when the point slipped in behind the edge of the glass. Gently turning the knife, the glass yielded and exposed a chink in the armour of about one sixteenth of an inch.

Then I remembered how, when I was a boy, I used to sniggle trout as they lay with noses upstream, fins idly fanning the water, basking in the watery sunlight that filtered down into the deep pools. With a little practice it was quite simple.

You slipped the rod point, with its tiny wire noose, into the water a little upstream and came down on the fish. If you missed him the first time you just let the wire brush past him and continue downstream for a bit. This way the trout was undisturbed, being quite used to twigs and weeds gliding past. Back upstream again, this time the noose is correctly guided over the trout's head. A quick jerk and there he goes sailing through the air in a flashing, flapping arc over your head.

I am glad now, that even in those early days, I soon dismissed this practice as being too easy and unfair. But I was thinking about it as I got a long piece of thin wire, and slipped it through the slit I had opened with my sgian dhubh.

Everyone watched breathlessly as the wire snaked out towards the dashboard. Once, twice, thrice it wove a tantalising circle round the key.

I had it! But, pull as I might, there it stayed, and I realised that I was trying to pull the key out at an angle. So I adopted a different tactic, giving the wire little, short, vibratory tugs. That did the trick.

Out came the key and danced about in mid-air. I dared hardly breathe as I slowly drew it towards me, and watched it flit crazily through the air, like a bee that has enjoyed, too well, the hospitality of the flowers and filled to capacity with nectar, weaves its way tipsily to the hive.

At long last the keyring appeared through the slit, but that wasn't all. The key remained stuck fast inside the car window. There just wasn't enough room for it to come out on the ring.

We weren't going to be beaten now. A big needle, a length of nylon fishing cast, a neat threading job, through the hole in the key and back. With a little hacksaw I cut the protruding metal circle and the keyring fell inside with a protesting tinkle. Then, like a practiced conjuror, I gently drew the looped nylon, and out came the key.

The American seized on it unbelievingly and opened the car. Without word he picked up his funny, little hat and popped it on his head, and did a whooping Indian war dance around his car.

Within a few days, a parcel arrived for the children from a thoughtful and thankful American who, I am sure, will never again lock himself out of his car.

Fashions! I follow their changing trends and marvel. Why, ladies, do you cast aside frilly femininity to draw on yards of suffocating material which creeps upwards to stretch protestingly across the beam?

In contrast, it is the men who go in for jolly pullovers that would make the Fair Isle dip smartly behind the horizon. Brilliant hues, churned out in hours of laborious knitting through the long, winter evenings, with fingers flying until the needles are red hot. The females have worked unstintingly for the men of their choice and the recipients, I am sure, having got over the first startled shock, stow them deeply away until holiday time, when they are worn brashly, under the cloak of anonymity.

People coming, people going, early and late. I think the record for early arrival was held by a party who came around 5.30 am.

My dear old Dad used to say, "If it is your wish to get anywhere, get up in the morning," and so I was 'on duty' and able to receive the early birds. After making their purchases they confessed that, unable to find hotel accommodation, they had spent the night in the car, and were cold and hungry.

Irralee was up and about by now, so we were able to offer them the hospitality of our fire, and it was good to see them come to life over their tea and hot scones, flanked by pats of fresh butter sitting cooly on a cabbage leaf, and a section of heather honey.

We made many friends, and each succeeding Christmas the chain of cards grew longer, and when the winds rattled the snow and hail against the windows of our little croft, we drew our chairs closer round the fire; and when the storm outside paused to take a breath before howling again we listened to the contented twittering of the little bats which had found a snug shelter in our roof.

We watched the glowing birch logs light up the painted robins, mistletoe, holly, and the words of good wishes that danced in the firelight and we thought of all those good friends who had remembered us.

9

Irralee's pullets were her pride and joy; a flock of her own breeding which had just come to maturity. They had achieved that maternal look and went out of their way to excite the attentions of the cockerel by showing off their flaming, scarlet combs and flaunting their saucy powder-puff bottoms. They crooned around the nest boxes like newly-weds and greeted the first eggs with the vociferous cackle of a group of maiden aunts.

But I had to admit there was something special about those eggs. They were beautifully shaped and the colour was a dark brown, inlaid with mahogany red. It would be a sin to crack such an egg into the degradation of a frying pan. The last rites it demanded were to be boiled lightly, timed meticulously, and enthroned in an eggcup in all its glory; to be approached tenderly, tapped gently on the crown and tasted between mouthfuls of home-baked bread and fresh butter. The albumen, white and light as thistledown, the yolk deep and rich denoting the unshackled bird with the freedom of the fields and woods and the goodness it has garnered there.

But freedom brings danger and I shared Irralee's concern when one of her flock went missing. I asked if they had been shut in last night and was assured they had been and, furthermore were all present and correct on being let out in the morning. The missing bird had not reported for its afternoon corn feed.

I was puzzled by this daylight robbery. It is usually in the quiet of the dawn or under cover of dusk that the foxes and wild cats strike. We searched all around and eventually found a small tuft of feathers and nearby, on the freshly upturned earth of a molehill, the single imprint of a big dog fox. I thought it was, indeed, a bold fellow to kill in the broad light of day and Irralee was frantic for the future safety of her pullets.

On my advice, she kept them shut in next day and I waited patiently with my gun, but there was no sign of a fox all morning and all I heard was the grousing of the locked-up birds. I stretched my cramped limbs and reported back to the house. We had a meal and afterwards I kicked off my brogues for a ten minute lounge in the big chair. Irralee was washing the dishes and her song was backed by an orchestration of clattering china.

The silence, when it came, swiped at me like a soft sandbag. I turned to see Irralee standing motionless, clutching the edge of the sink, her gaze transfixed through the kitchen window. Her lips were moving, but not a word came forth. I was wondering what on earth was wrong when Irralee declared, in a strained, husky voice,

"He's outside the window watching me".

I sprinted to the door in my stocking feet, the gun leapt into my hand as I passed it and I raced round the house. The fox and I met, in near collision, I with a gasp, the fox with a snarl. In that split second I pointed my gun and fired from the hip.

It was a big dog fox that had seen more than his share of frosty mornings, and his fangs were worn down with age. This, then was the reason for the daylight raids. The old fox, no longer fit to catch the fleet, wild creatures turned to poultry for easier pickings.

I thought Irralee would have been delighted with the passing of her hen-killer, but with the perversity of the fair sex, she stood over the fox's body.

"He looks nice, doesn't he?"

"No, he doesn't", said I.

But, unhearing, Irralee went on, "I suppose I betrayed him, when all the time he was just sitting there looking at me".

I could feel the sob coming.

"Look", I said, with the agitated savagery of a male trying to defend his actions, "do you really want to know what that mean old thing was doing outside the window? He was there to enquire when the devil you were going to let the birds out."

That started us both laughing. Then Irralee, with a typically feminine switch, became all practical. "There's a bounty on the brush".

"Oh, we won't bother about that", I said. "We'll just give him a decent burial".

But Irralee persisted. "The money will buy another box of cartridges".

I was emphatic.

"It would mean going to the Police Station, and I never, never go near a Police Station!"

As I knocked on the coldly, official door I wondered what I would say, but when the tall figure in blue appeared he said, "You have a brush there. Come in."

As I toddled after him towards the inevitable form-filling, I marvelled at the powers of our police. How did he know what was in the brown paper parcel tucked under my arm? I took a quick look and there dangling out of the bottom corner, was a good six inches of the fox's tail.

It was not long after the fox episode that Irralee's pullets took another knock. One of the birds had gone 'all expectant' and had been given some eggs to sit on. In due course, nature waved her miraculuous wand, out popped the chickens and everyone was happy.

That is, happy until one evening, when Irralee went to shut the little coop for the night. It was then she noticed the chickens scattered far and wide, 'peeping' forlornly and, of their mother, nothing but a tattered matt of feathers. I followed the pathetic trail until the feathers thinned out to an odd downy tuft and then the darkness beat me. The chickens spent the night on top of the hot water tank.

Next morning I moved the chicken coop to within a few yards of the house for safety and we spent a long time trying to persuade a half-hearted hen to adopt the orphans. She wasn't thoroughly convinced that full family responsibilities descended just as suddenly as that! Being a mere male I left

Irralee and the hen to it and set off to check the cattle.

That evening I returned to find the reluctant mother gone, a distraught Irralee and the chickens back on the hot water tank.

Next morning I borrowed a good, reliable broody hen from a neighbour and the chickens were introduced to their third mother. I took up a concealed position near the coop, knowing that if I did not see this through tonight, it would have to be tomorrow, or the day after that. I was so stiff and sore that I longed for the warmth of the fireside and the comfort of the big chair.

With the darkening came a whispering sound, just like the wind sprites as they prepare for a wild race to whip up the waters and shake the tree tops. Through the gloom came a large, shuffling bear-like shadow. With a deep grunt it bounded forward.

Later I skinned the big, boar badger with grim satisfaction, Irralee's chickens would live now, and, once I had cured this magnificent skin, it would make up into the finest badger sporran I had ever worn.

Normally badgers are quiet, peace-loving, nocturnal animals and don't bother us and we, in return, do not molest them. Indeed, I can remember having the warmest feelings for one that cleaned out all the jackdaws' nests one spring on Creag Mhor.

But I felt this old rogue was fortunate too. Not for him the ultimate end, to rot in the bowels of the earth. He would outlive them all! sporting his creamy, striped head at the ceilidhs, getting his soft, tufted ears twiddled as he lay in my lap through committee meetings. Would he not always be to the forefront when I led a Highland bull in the pedigree sale ring?

On a night out he would become my guardian and my exchequer and if I were to dip too frequently into his breast, his jaw would gently close over my hand and, like an old friend, lead me out, onto the road for home.

I know all young things have a special appeal — puppies,

kittens, chickens, calves, foals etc., but I found the most fascinating of all were ducklings. To me, they almost had a human touch, the wish to love and belong.

This sense seems to be instinctive from the moment they emerge from the egg, and is most apparent in the spring on the loch when sometimes a late-hatching duckling is left behind, or a very young duckling takes a wrong turning. Then, the late arrival or lost one will 'peep-peep' all over the place searching for someone or something to belong to and, should it find you in these moments, will stick like glue.

I can remember being on the loch in the big boat, powered with the outboard engine, and as I passed the island a young duckling suddenly shot out and pursued the boat. Desperately its tiny feet spanked across the top of the water, its little wings beat the air like harnessed butterflies and its beak kept opening and shutting, like a squawking, mechanical toy.

I had to stop and pick it up and eventually found the mother and the rest of the brood a good half mile away, which lost me an afternoon's fishing.

With the help of a hen I reared some ducklings of my own. I was left to do most of the rearing as the hen was never enchanted by her charges, and when they found our little burn they dashed to its gurgling music like the children of Hamelin. For a long time the hen frantically paced the bank and tried to call the ducklings back.

At one point I thought she was going to lift her feathered skirts and wade in, but the chill of the water decided her against it. She took a last look at her unruly youngsters and ran away to rejoin her own kind. I'm sure she never went broody again and swore off maternity for ever.

The ducklings never seemed to miss their foster-mother and pattered round my feet, cocking their heads to one side and looking up with liquid, trusting eyes. In my experience, it is only the 'duckling' that does this and never the 'drakeling'.

When they grew bigger and ready to take their first dip in the loch I went with them, to see that they got there and back safely, and would know their way next time. All went well until they reached the spot where the burn mouth yawned into the loch and I was thoroughly enjoying their antics in the deep water. They dived, splashed and bobbed about like animated corks, when suddenly one of the little ducks disappeared in a swirl of water, as if snatched down by an unseen hand.

The others fluttered to the safety of the bank in a panic-stricken rush, where I gathered together my little flock and waited hopefully, anxiously, then despairingly. I waited for it to bob up with an 'all's well' quack, but it never did and, sorrowfully, I drove the rest home.

But I wasted no time in regret, and contacted Paddy, who was in the district on his annual holiday.

Paddy was a nice young fellow and the girls were always after him, but Paddy, who had hardly given marriage serious thought, remained a determined bachelor and evaded all feminine tactics by going fishing. And he was a fisherman plus!

He spent all his spare time, weekends and holidays in pursuit of trout and salmon so there wasn't a trick on the water or a lure that he didn't know.

That afternoon I told Paddy my story. We both agreed that a large predatory monster of some kind lay at the bottom near the burn mouth, and we planned our attack.

We set sail in the big boat with tackle that would have tethered a horse and large treble-hooked baits the size and shape of a herring. We called them 'Krushchevs' because they were a vivid red and carried the most formidable iron-mongery.

Out in the loch we set the heavy rods up, one on either side of the boat, threw the baits overboard and watched them spin attractively in the water to disappear as the lines ran out. Twenty, thirty, forty yards, the boat purring quietly, we towed them along the bottom of the loch.

We made the mouth of the burn in a long, curving sweep, trailing our baits through the little bay and across the fatal spot where the duckling had vanished. Tensely we watched the rods, but nothing happened. I turned the boat round and made another run from a different direction.

This time I edged the boat into the lochside as near as I dared without fouling the propeller. So close, in fact, that Paddy was in a sweat lest we hang up the baits on an underwater rock or tree root. Over the bay again. If my calculations were right the baits should be skimming nicely towards the spot. I nudged the boat closer still and shut the engine back to crawling point.

A reel shrieked and we nearly jumped out of our skins. One of the rods leapt over the stern of the boat and I just caught the butt as it passed me. The rod bucked wildly in my hands, I let out the last five yards of line and shut off the engine.

"There now," said Paddy, "I told you we would catch one of those tree roots."

To me, it was like an underwater lorry going in the opposite direction and I asked Paddy to take the rod. It bent like a withy in his hands, and his eyes assumed the proportions of searchlights as the 'tree root' started to take us in tow! I slipped the oars into the rowlocks and started to ease the strain. Our tackle was good, but I felt it must be reaching its limit.

Paddy was always so cool and unruffled whilst playing big fish that I found myself enjoying the spectacle he now presented. His face was as red as a turkey cock and little rivulets trickled down his temples as he 'pumped' the rod strenuously and wound in some hard won line, only to have it snatched away again. This went on for about half an hour, during which time Paddy was reduced to the quality of a limp rag.

"Oh, Paddy!" I said, as seriously as I could, "Now that I remember, this is where somebody ditched their old car."

"If they did," stuttered Paddy, "they left the bloody engine running. Here have a shot at this, maybe it'll knock some of the nonsense out of you."

He was right. After ten minutes of heaving and pulling I wasn't in such a funny frame of mind, but after a further spell of frantic 'reeling in' we both got our first look at what was on the end.

The gloom of the water was lit up by a moving mass of shimmering bronzes, up and up it came, getting bigger and bigger and then, just below the surface, it rolled over showing a gaping mouth with rows of cruel teeth and a long white belly, which slid down into the depths again like a diving submarine.

Paddy was breathing down my neck.

"A flaming shark," he hissed, and I agreed. To call it a pike would have been to libel a fish of this size.

"If he gets his jaw across that line," said Paddy, "he's away. Can I have another go?"

I was only too happy to hand over and knew the monster couldn't be in safer hands. One wrong move and it would get those teeth across the wire trace and snip it like a piece of thread. In the next moment an awful thought struck me.

"Paddy," I gabbled, "I've forgotten to bring the gaff. We'll never land it without one."

Paddy, intent on the last stages of the battle, never looked round, but he heard me all right and croaked,

"In my bag, there's a telescopic one. In my bag!"

I fumbled amongst the paraphernalia at the bottom of the boat and pulled at the metal gaff. I yanked it to its full length, examined the deadly hook and took up my stance. The water boiled as Paddy expertly piloted the monster towards the boat. I held my breath to steady myself and, as the huge bulk slid past me, I leaned over the side and struck with everything I had, and held on.

Paddy was at my side, and together we heaved the massive, flapping fish into the boat. The big pike nearly filled the bottom of the boat and we were both forced to take evasive action by perching on the bow and stern, respectively, drawing our legs clear of the threshing body and snapping jaws.

If there are doubts about St George and the Dragon, I, personally, can vouch for Paddy and the monster. For it was he, who, with daring dash, delivered the 'coup de grace'. I thought of how all the fishes and wild life of the loch must have rejoiced in that moment, and as I took my axe and chopped my way along the five feet of monster I figured that these big fish steaks would feed the hens for at least a fortnight. They did, and Irralee declared that the hens never laid better.

The ducklings soon reached the 'flapper' stage and the upturned glance was blended with a delicate coyness. As fully fledged ducks I got the 'head on the side' direct gaze. It registered unfettered fidelity, mellowed experience too. They had also found their voices, a rich, resonant 'quack, quack'. At this stage the drakes never got beyond clearing their throats.

The ducks were very fussy about time and laid their eggs with machinelike precision. If I reported at the correct hour in the morning, (eight o'clock) and opened the duck house door, they would leisurely emerge, one by one, giving me the fond upward look, 'plop' into the burn and commence an unhurried, meticulous toilet, and inside the house were the eggs.

If I were too early they would stick their heads out of the door, with the discomforted air of ladies disturbed in a powder room session and, at least one, would lodge her protest by laying her egg in the burn. On the other hand, if I were late, they would come out with a great hustle and bustle. If they could spare the time I would be thrown a mild, reproachful look. A hurried make-do 'splash-and-a-promise' and they were on their way, shooting the rapids, guddling in the pools and on, down to the burn mouth.

This, despite their early experience, was the ducks' favourite spot and they happily whiled away the hours, splashing, diving, preening, with an occasional forty winks, heads tucked cosily under their wings, rocked by the ripples of the loch. Then they would work their way up the burn again and arrive back at the duck house in time for their evening meal, after which they retired inside to a bed of bracken to sleep the night away in comfort and in safety.

As a shepherd knows his flock, so I knew my ducks, despite their similarity in appearance, size and dress. And, on this particular night I knew it was Finoola who hadn't reported for her evening meal. I searched down the burn, hoping that perhaps she had found some tasty guddling spot and was loathe to leave it. But I found myself back at the burn mouth, wondering if, after all this time, another monster had come to torment me.

Sitting down on a large stone, I gazed moodily across the water when, to my amazement, a pair of smouldering eyes gazed back at me for a brief second then disappeared without so much as a ripple on the deep water.

That night I went to consult the Oracle on nature subjects, the old gamekeeper. I finally tracked him down in the kitchen of the local hotel, where I found him engaged in counting the crystal drops that he carefully released from the tap to join the amber liquid in his glass. He looked up from this delicate operation in response to my question.

"Yon", he said, "is a big, sea otter, which *I*", and he emphasised the word, "tried to catch last year when he took old Meg's pet Aylesbury".

I ventured my own plan.

"What about a bait trap at the mouth of the burn?" The old man's scorn died as it was born.

"Laddie", he said gently, "you'll never catch an otter that way. Least of all that big fellow" and he turned back to his glass.

Despite this, next morning I set my trap with all the cunning I knew. By early afternoon I could contain myself no longer and returned to have a look. My trap, with its tempting bait of fresh rabbit, was untouched. But nearby I noticed a mound of freshly-chopped rushes, and underneath, the body of a water-rail. I felt sure that the otter had slain the bird when he wasn't hungry, meaning to return later so carefully I set my trap at the kill.

The wild geese, silhouetted in the moonlight, sent the frosty air vibrating with their wingbeats, as I paid my final visit to the loch. A noise like a runaway steam engine greeted me and the sharp click of teeth just inches away, told me that my wildest hopes had been realised!

I could see the red, glowing eyes switch on and off at the slightest movement, and the flash of ivory teeth as his lips rose and fell. A terrible silence prevailed as we faced each other. Those penetrating eyes asked no quarter, but just a chance to get to grips. The powerful muscles waited for my next move. I had the feeling that this big otter and I were the only living things on Earth — and I did not want to be alone.

Slipping softly backwards I cut a stout, forked hazel stick, with a swift rush forwards I completely surprised my adversary and pinned him, by the neck, to the ground. I inched my foot forward until it rested on the spring of the trap, and, as I leant my weight forward, the forepaw was released.

Feeling his freedom, this bundle of electrified muscle, bounded upward and the end of the stick, catching me squarely on the chest, hurled me on my back. Thus, I saw my quarry plunge over me and away into the night.

My chest hurt a bit as I turned homeward and I suddenly felt very tired and cold; my steps, like my thoughts, a little uncertain. I would never now be able to boast to the old gamekeeper of my capture. But, in time, the otter repaid the bill he owed, by never bothering my ducks again.

In late October the children always organised the annual hazel nut expedition, and we set out for the woods complete with sacks to gather supplies for the winter. I was always taken along as 'Shaker-in-Chief'. The tree-shaking, to the youngsters, was more than half the fun. They knew every nut tree and gathered around each in turn.

Then I was required to climb half way up, grasp the centre of the tree and shake it with everything I could give. If it was a good tree, and a good year, the nuts would shower down like outsize hailstones and the children squeal their protests as the nuts rapped them smartly on the head. But I knew they really appreciated this, and had a poor opinion of any tree that did not 'bomb' them.

After that, there was a free-for-all good natured scramble

to pick up the fallen nuts, pop them into the sacks, and on to the next tree to repeat the whole performance.

The best nut year I remember, was one when we visited only half a dozen trees and found ourselves laden with a sufficiency for Christmas, the New Year, and a lot more besides. The children returned in a surge of excited chatter, their sacks filled to overflowing, and goodness knows how many more being consumed on their way home.

I stayed behind to fix a salt lick on one of the trees where the cattle would be able to reach up and run their tongues over it. I had just finished the job when a jay swept over my head, shrieking in gutteral abuse. Whilst in the woods, the swearing of the red squirrels rose to a crescendo of full-blooded cursing.

I thought I heard a movement in a matted blanket of copper-tinted bracken to my right, and for a brief moment two wicked eyes look out. Below them dangled the body of a squirrel — then nothing.

Two days later Irralee went to inspect the nest of a hen that was laying away, under a juniper bush on the hill. She found the hen twitching her last, cleanly and efficiently despatched by a single bite which had broken her neck, we never saw the killer, but it cannot have been short of victims, or food, as it never returned to claim the body of the hen. I couldn't help feeling that this event was somehow coupled with the pair of eyes and the limp, pathetic body of the squirrel.

The next to go was Charity. At least we liked to think it was her. Charity was one of three partridges which, at this time of year, picked up their living around the croft. You have probably guessed the other two.

I was coming off the hill one day with a rabbit for the pot when, in a powdering of snow, I saw two bright red spots and four feathers. Charity had received her last donation — death. I thought, at first, it had come from the sky as the surrounding snow was unmarked, but about ten feet away I found where the killer had crouched and gathered itself for that terrific spring. I went back to the fatal spot again and six feet in the other direction. This was where the beast had landed, not such a big jump this time, but a good effort with Charity in its jaws.

I followed the tell-tale trail up the hill, swung round some big rocks and sought cover in a large heap of logs. I cast a wide circle around. The snow was virgin and unmarked. It was in there — with Charity!

I slid the safety catch off my gun, slipped quietly forward and gave the logs a resounding thump with my brogue. Like a jack-in-a-box a head shot up out of the timber and looked me straight in the face. I have never been treated to such a cold, calculating gaze.

The pine marten slid its long, lithe body out of the logs, turned almost casually and looked at me again with jet black eyes that glittered in the warm russet fur and a long cream throat tinted with delicate flame. Never have I seen anything so cruelly beautiful and I could not bring myself to shoot.

Sometimes I find it hard to follow the intricate pattern of nature's plan, as she poises the peregrine falcon to plummet down on the fleeing red grouse; provides the rabbit that the wild cat rends to share with her growling, snarling kittens; and sends the golden eagle to pluck the blue hare from the mountain top. This magnificent devil was part of that plan.

As I watched the marauder vanish in three lightning leaps I felt privileged to have met the rare pine marten. Oh, by the way, Faith and Hope fully justified their names and survived to rear a fat, little brood of fourteen.

The casualties among the wild birds found their way from time to time to the sanctuary of Croft Douglas. There was the unconscious robin; how tenderly it was tucked into a blanket of cottonwool in a chocolate box and placed on the hot water tank. How good to hear the squeals of delight when the redbreast was found, next morning, perched on the edge of the goldfish bowl apparently none the worse.

Another time a frozen tomtit spent two nights with us, roosting on a set of antlers, like a little powder puff stuffed with breadcrumbs and suet; then there were the pheasant chicks we had such a hard job persuading a hen to foster, after their mother had fallen a victim to grinding wheels on the road. But one morning I thought I had a larger casualty to deal with. Just past the Queen's View I saw a large bird in the middle of the road, I stopped the car and got out. It was a hen capercailzie and as I approached she just sat still. I wondered if she had damaged herself on the telphone wires as she surveyed me with a not unfriendly eye, and raised the feathers on the back of her neck like a broody hen.

She was, too! a host of little heads popped out at intervals from her breast feathers. I gave the bird a good talking to, about the middle of the road being no place to brood her newly-hatched chicks and, as I hustled the family off the highway into the friendly shelter of fern and bracken, I sighed for a camera to catch this moment. I had never before seen the little ones bobbing about like multi-coloured blooms in the first hour of their birth.

The casualty who had the longest stay with us was Iain, or, to give him his full name Iain Dubh (Black Ian). He was a young raven who had tumbled from his nest high up on the crags of Creag Mhor, and landed in a fluttering heap at the bottom, to attract our attention by croaking forlornly and incessantly.

I stuffed the squawking bundle of black feathers into a bag and made a perilous attempt to climb the face of the rock and return him to his nest. I could see the nest quite plainly, the base of its structure was formed by stout interlocking tree branches, and I knew that a raven could never have picked up the lightest of these boughs, let alone fly with it to the top of this peak.

This was an old eyrie; built and abandoned by the golden eagle, the ravens had moved in. There was another young raven in there and I could see the movement of its head as it peeped, full of curiosity, over the edge of the eyrie.

Should I leave the young raven on this narrow ledge? I knew that the old birds weren't far away. They circled high above me, like two black smudges writing their anxiety in the sky. They would feed and care for the youngster, but the wild cat would have no trouble in climbing as high as I had, and would lick her chops over such a tasty snack.

At this moment my mind was made up for me. The youngster in the nest let out a raucous shriek to be answered from my bag with a muffled croak, and one of the parents, in a menacing dive, almost swept me from my perch. That settled it. I retired as hastily as I could and Iain Dubh was installed in the stable at Croft Douglas.

Feeding him was, at first, quite a problem. He wouldn't pick up anything and ignored the tasty pieces of chopped liver. We tried prising open his beak to slip in a piece of meat, but to no avail. Iain just spat it out and sat back, blinking stupidly.

Next, I tried the natural approach and treated him to some fullblooded, deepthroated croaks. Iain's reactions were immediate. He screeched excitedly and I found myself staring down his ample gullet, so I popped a piece of liver straight down. This procedure was repeated half a dozen times till Iain squatted down in the manger and blinked slowly and contentedly.

The young raven grew rapidly and had a finger, or rather a feather, in everything that went on around Croft Douglas. He surveyed the feeding of the hens and the milking of the house cow, and would sit in the doorway of the byre until the milking was finished always hoping to beat the cat in a wild race for the saucerful of milk. It was usually a draw and they sipped and swore at each other.

Iain was also a great mimic. He would mew softly and call the kittens, then chuckle in delight at their bewilderment. He could also cluck with the laying hens, copy the crowing of the cock and bark like a dog.

Tarra and he became great friends and, together, they herded everything, kittens, hens and ducks. But when Tarra was called upon to round up some invading sheep Iain was hard put to keep it up, and hopped, flapped and puffed until, in a moment of despair, he spread his wings and, to his own amazement, floated effortlessly. From that moment he directed all proceedings from the air.

One day, when I saw Iain rise replete from a rabbit carcase he had found I knew he had acquired the priceless asset of independence and that it was time for him to return to his own element and kind. I popped him into a bag (he needed a much bigger one this time) and made for the creag, right back to the old eyrie. I held Iain a moment, gave him my blessing and threw him into the air. As he circled the crags I quickly disappeared, lest he should be tempted to follow me back to the croft.

A week later I revisited the eyrie but all was quiet and I was watching a kestrel hawk, delicately suspended above me, when it screamed and dived straight down the cliff face. A black shape hurtled towards me. It was Iain. He landed a few feet from me and danced around, then, with a sweep of his great wings rose again sweeping round and round my head, croaking with pleasure at our meeting.

I knew it was not my place to linger and so weaken the links that now bound Iain to the wild and, as he tilted a wing gracefully I waved back a fond farewell. On the way home I reflected that I had never seen a bird sporting such polished plumage, and was sure that the cow's milk must take the credit.

Every February, when the ravens return to Creag Mhor to inspect the nesting sites, they treat us to a great display of aerobatics. There is a large cock bird who outflies them all and who can execute to perfection the ravens' aerial speciality — sweeping down in a powerful dive, pulling out to level up, fold his wings and leisurely roll over.

I like to think it is Iain, reared on liver and cow's milk and I think, too, of the line,

"He who feeds the raven, will aye be fed and cled".

10

At an appointed time each year the cattle were rounded up and herded into the cattle pens to undergo a compulsory Tuberculin test. This was just a matter of form as far as the Highlanders were concerned and, when one of the calves, which had never known the touch of a human hand, 'exploded' at the jag of the needle, the exasperated vet was heard to exclaim,

"As if a T.B. germ would ever hope to 'licht' on that!"

It was at this time, too, that we tattooed the ears of the new calves with their pedigree and registration numbers; a day that always dawned at the height of the tourist season, and one that the prophets marked as a holiday as neither they, nor anyone else, knew exactly what was going to happen.

The penned cattle drew the crowds of visitors like a giant magnet and they moved in from all directions. Camera shutters whirred, clicked and chattered like a battery of whispering machine guns, which did nothing to soothe the mounting nervousness among the cattle. The cows growled, as only Highland cattle can; they knew full well what awaited them in the catching crate at the end of the pens — the vet reeking of disinfectant, armed with twin guns that stabbed, in quick successsion, and spat under their hides, the liquid that searched for a tuberculin reaction. It was enought to make the hair of any self-respecting Highlander stand on end!

But proceedings, on this occasion, were held up before the vet arrived. I had noticed a young heifer with a swollen mouth that would have to be examined. The ropes went into action and, in a whirl of dust, the beastie was haltered and tied.

Was it a snake bite? That would be unusual as snakes were almost unknown on our hill, although Schiehallion used to be the home of the adders. It is said that wild goats were introduced for the purpose of dealing with the snakes and that the goats, with their hatred of reptiles, used their sharp, flint-like feet to good effect and literally 'stamped out' the adders.

The shepherds viewed, with great misgivings, the billies' amorous advances toward the blackface ewes, and a goat chop made a change from venison.

But it wasn't a snake bite that troubled the heifer. One of her teeth was wedged round and cut deeply into her lip. This

was probably the result of an accidental kick in the face during some 'high jinks' with the other youngsters. There was only one solution — the tooth would have to come out.

Irralee held the heifer's mouth open and I had the pliers poised to make the extraction when a coachload of visitors arrived. There was nothing we could do about it but get on with the job. I'm sure no dentist had such a vast audience and a long-drawn 'aah' greeted the reappearance of the pliers with the offending tooth. A South African gold miner begged for the tooth as a souvenir and treated it with the reverence due to a nugget!

The testing was almost at an end. I was always so glad when this moment was arrived at, the moment with no one regretting having taken part.

Our neighbours from Chamberbane, Foss and Drumnakyle, always came so willingly to lend a hand at 'the testing' and I dreaded that they would go away with a bad impression, like a dig in the ribs with a horn that had a ton of beef behind it. But all had gone so smoothly and I was ushering the last beast through the pens to the all-embracing cattle crush, the tight unforgiving regulations and the inevitable needle. This was the youngest heifer with a name in Gaelic akin to dynamite. I should have been warned!

Someone called for a light and I raised my eyes to watch the box of matches float effortlessly through the air. In this second I learned yet another lesson. Never, never ever take your eye off the animal you are shepherding.

The kick came, a wicked backlash with the leg at full stretch. I had been kicked many times before and had long ago learned that to stay close to the offending animal was the safest place. But now, in an unguarded moment, I had been caught. It was a savage blow, delivered with the sharp crack of a snapping stick, a blow that did not warrant a shout or shriek to advertise the pain involved, but one that sent me kneeling to the ground, gasping, moaning and groaning, to myself. The last spasms, the final contortions that carried with them the pain-killing hiss had barely left me when

Irralee dashed on the scene and, on seeing my plight but observing that I was 'coming round' commiserated briefly and announced with her special brand of machine-gun fire.

"There's a gentleman from the Ministry of Agriculture to see you".

I hobbled painfully to meet him and he hopped and hobbled, with a practised gait, to meet me. A man well seasoned by the condiments of life, he had long ago taken out an insurance against the elements of surprise. He was the 'subsidy puncher' of hill calves, and surveyed me as if my time on earth were soon to be terminated.

"You have been kicked".

I nodded dumbly.

"Where?"

"On my knee", I managed to croak.

The Puncher shook his head with a solemn deliberation. "I thought as much. I got it in the very same place five years ago" and, shamelessly, he pulled up his trouser leg to display a horrible, hairy, atrophied limb. Now he announced dramatically,

"I am crippled for life", and, pausing to savour the moment of having a companion to travel a similar hippety-hoppety road, added in satisfactory tones, "so will you be".

I inwardly vowed that I would not give the Puncher the pleasure of my company in his hopalong existence. The strength of my resolve saw me, within the week 'sound in wind and limb' as the vet would have put it.

It was not often we called in the vet. This action warranted a serious situation indeed and, like every important moment in life, the hands of the clock meticulously ticked off the seconds of decision. I had another look at An Nighean Righ (The Princess), one of our favourite and most valuable heifers. She had the look that said, apologetically,

"I am not well".

I knew she was serious and needed skilled help.

The vet arrived in a cloud of dust and an excruciating scream of brakes. He was the fastest and most daring driver in the district and many a cow owed her life to his breakneck speeding when she couldn't rise from 'the staggers' and a life-saving injection gave her the chance to look upon another day.

You only had to see the vet in your driving mirror to give him immediate right of way. He had no blue, flashing, howling bleeper, but just the cold, calculating message that his journey was really necessary. Like his driving, he was always direct and to the point.

"I think", he said, "she has been poisoned. Keep her moving around and drench every hour with treacle and water, and call me if she is no better".

So saying, he leapt into his iron horse, leaving behind, hanging like a deadly speck in the air, the word 'poison'. I was almost sure now of its origin.

It is said that the only animals that will eat ragwort is the sheep. We had no sheep and pulled the offending weed by hand and always tried to dispose, in a safe place, of the 'weebies', as they are locally known and after a 'pulling session' when the air and your hands were tainted with their acrid smell, they earned their full title of 'Stinking Willie'. And stink they did, but in their dying had a determination to spite the earth and everything that fed upon it and, with a deceit that drew the innocent, turned to a black, decaying mass which suddenly became extremely palatable and deadly poisonous.

The Princess had found such a meal and fallen to temptation.

This was a family affair and everyone was literally 'roped in', to the rescue. The young ones, with their heels dug determinedly into the turf held the end of the halter to secure and steady the heifer's head with a confidence that we were wordlessly giving them. Irralee had prepared a bucket of the brew and with the cool calmness of femininity in a crisis, she deftly poured the first measure into a milk bottle.

I looked at my beautiful heifer and was at a loss for words. What does one say to a princess when you are pouring treacle and water down her reluctant throat?

The air was filled with foreboding. The sky darkened to an ominous shade of deep purple. Suddenly there was a tremendous flash of lightning and the hills shook with a thunderous roar. I don't know how he managed it, but the Devil had clawed his way, cloud after cloud, into the heavens and was now tearing the place apart with a fiendish delight. He tossed hissing, fizzing, exploding catherine wheels around the peaks of Schiehallion, Faragon and Creag-an-loch, then extended his fiery fingers to send the lightning in a deadly dance over the waters of the loch and leaned down and banged the heads of the hills together.

As if this were not enough, he played his final card, a spectacular effort guaranteed to strike fear into the stoutest heart — a gigantic fireball. He tossed it down almost carelessly, and it swept its fiery way towards us, growing bigger and bigger until we could see its hungry flames licking its spinning sides. It crashed into an oak tree not fifty yards from us. It seemed so close, and my hand shook as I held the bottle. One of the young ones gave a stifled sob.

"Not to worry", I said, with a lightheartedness that I did not feel. "That old Devil is just trying to scare us with his tricks".

"Yes," said Irraleee, "and he's going to get into deep trouble for all the mischief he's making".

With that, the rain came down in torrents of solid water. In seconds we were soaked to the skin. Irralee, her sodden hair like a tangle of seaweed, raised her pale, gleaming face to the sky.

"There", she said, with a conviction I had to marvel at, "that's God throwing buckets of water over that old Devil and his firecrackers".

The little heads nodded silently in approval, and we allowed ourselves a family chuckle. Even the heifer looked better, or we liked to think she did, so we bade her good-night and squelched our way back to the house where everyone was stripped off, dried out and sat around the fire wrapped in blankets, sipping steaming cups of cocoa and laughing over the fate of the Devil.

To this day, thunder and lightning bring no fear to our family, but only the memory of our desperate attempts to save The Princess at the height of a storm.

The dawn brought another call to the vet. He left us with a needle, syringe and the appropriate doses to be injected at two hourly intervals. The Princess was a big, strong heifer, carrying her first calf. Even in her illness she maintained a majesty of posture and when pain was present never let it be known. I searched for the spot on her warm, hairy hide, with a determination to follow the vet's instructions to the letter.

How I felt for The Princess as I stabbed the needle home, but she never flinched as I pumped the contents of the syringe into her system and I prayed it would annihilate the poisonous demons which sought to destroy her.

After a night, when the mattress felt hard, the blankets heavy and the pillow uncomfortable and unkind, I heard the cock crow and dragged myself wearily from the bed. There was a calmness in the dawn and no need for the last of the needle and the syringe. The heifer, which had so bravely and silently fought for her life, had lowered her head as if the crown of horns she wore proudly, now weighed just a bit too much, and kissed the earth a last farewell.

The Princess was dead.

In our grief we could not allow ourselves the luxury of mourning over our tragic loss and when the truck called to take away the body I was paid the current price for a 'fallen animal'. One pound! I gazed at the note in disbelief. This was all that was left of our valuable heifer and friend. It was a big shock for our finances and our way of life, just when everything seemed to be going our way. But the situation had to be faced up to, our herd number had to be maintained and there was now this unexpected vacancy.

Advertised in the local paper was a sale of Pedigree Highland Cattle. I went resolutely to the chest of drawers in the bedroom and took out my dress dirk. It was a chieftain's weapon; crowning the big blade a delicately cut cairngorm glowed warmly, but a touch told of its ice cold reality; my finger traced the celtic pattern engraved on the sheath of silver, where snugly lay the silver knife and fork, the insignia of one who was above eating with his fingers. It was a prized possession, but I consoled myself with the thought that, when times were better, I would replace it.

It was a busy day in town. I had intended to look around the market pens to assess the animals on offer. I never got past the first pen. She was magnificent, one of the largest framed cows I had ever seen. A quick consultation with the catalogue told me her name, Mairi of Glenfinnan. Her owner was there.

"We have to sell. We are moving from the croft."

"What sort of price are you expecting?" I asked, tentatively.

"Oh," he said, with all the confidence in the world, "she'll make a hundred and thirty, a hundred and forty guineas."

I did a swift piece of calculation. Pedigree Highland cattle were sold in guineas and I had to watch the extra shillings in the pound.

I made my way back to the centre of the city. A large placard in a shop window said,

'Silver and Gold, bought and sold.'

The door bell tinkled out my arrival and I laid the dress dirk on the velvet cloth on the counter. It felt like, and was, the moment of sacrifice. I watched the delicate fingers appraising it and raised my eyes to meet the pale, dark framed face that betrayed not a flicker of emotion and a voice that announced in stentorian tones,

"One hundred pounds, that is our top offer."

I picked up my dirk and made for the door. The deep, dark brown voice halted me,

"What is it you want?"

"I need", I said, with the courage of desperation, "one hundred and fifty pounds."

Not another word was exchanged as I watched the fine hands counting out the notes, one hundred and fifty pounds.

I rushed back to the market just as the sale was beginning and, in no time at all, Mairi was in the ring. She had a fascinating step, as though she were wishing to go dancing and the sawdust flew up joyfully from the tune of her feet.

"Two hundred. One hundred, then." Just to start with the auctioneer had a condescending tone. I waved my hand.

"One hundred guineas" but, immediately, my bid was topped. I waved again, and again I was overruled. With a desperate calculation I made my final bid.

"I am bid one hundred and fifty pounds", chanted the auctioneer.

I prayed silently and earnestly that my unknown opponent would yield, and longed to explain to him just what it was all about. The waiting of the last few seconds was agony. Once, twice, then the sound that was a blend of decision and finality and the final smack of the auctioneer's hammer.

"Sold to Croft Douglas." They knew me there.

On the way home I sang contentedly, the words of the song 'Mairi's Wedding',

"Plenty herring, plenty meal,
Plenty bonnie bairns as weel,
That's the toast for Mairi."

Her arrival and happy-go-lucky nature were just the tonic we needed at Croft Douglas. She settled as if she had been there all her life and Mairi had a secret, not disclosed at the sale. She had indeed been wed and, to prove it, presented us, within a month of her arrival, a big, beautiful, heifer calf. What a wonderful feeling it is to climb the peak of ecstasy after wallowing in the mire of despair. We sang, we danced and rejoiced, we had a heifer back and big Mairi as well.

She was the biggest Highland cow I had ever seen and calving made not a whit of difference to her dimensions. Loaded with milk, her udder almost trailed the turf, but her calf proved to be a 'sleepy one' (they say you get human ones with the same affliction). This big calf made a half-hearted attempt to do what nature commanded and find out where the nourishment was. It searched vaguely along Mairi's enormous flank and even under her tail, then gave up and lay down.

I was exasperated. Hunger, I thought, will solve everything, but it didn't. Three days and the calf hadn't supped a drop and Mairi's bag was getting swollen and hard, resembling the biggest set of bagpipes ever seen in Strathtummel.

It was time for action and we herded Mairi and her offspring into the catching pens. The calf, by now was teetering weakly. There is a saying about 'taking the bull by the horns' but, with the calf wedged tightly between my knees, I took big Mairi by the teat. The highland lady, not unnaturally, took a very poor view of this and made a lunge at me with a deadly, scything sweep of her horns. The left one glided up the sleeve of my jacket, the point shearing neatly through the material at the elbow.

Still clutching the calf I twisted my body and quickly slipped off what remained of my jacket which, by a stroke of luck, wound itself around Mairi's head, momentarily blinding her. I seized the chance and squeezed the fat, milk-filled teat that I was holding and squirted some of its creamy contents over the calf's muzzle and popped the teat into its mouth. As the calf latched on I disengaged the jacket from Mairi's horn and watched her gaze admiringly at her little one, down on its knees, which was already reducing the size of her bag.

As I left the blissful scene, the slurp, slurping of the sucking calf made the sweetest of music to my ears.

11

June is not a month to fish Loch Tummel. It is the time when trout laze indolently on the bottom, or playfully glide and 'plop' on the surface, with a flash of a dorsal fin and gleaming, twisting tail as they roll gently over.

All the latest types of spinning lure, conceived with the greatest cunning to dive and wriggle in the most realistic way, the very top flight of fishy temptresses, cause not the flutter of a scale down below. On the surface every variety of fly that was ever tied, in every colour of the rainbow, from the size of a fledgling to the tiniest nymph, no matter how skilfully placed or manoeuvered are all disdainfully ignored or, at best, fastidiously 'nosed'. This, I think, is done by the experienced to expose the concealed barb to the curious young fry.

It was at this time of year that our oldest, Maureen, announced, with an unblinking stare of her blue eyes, that she had promised to take to school next morning a trout, which was to be the chief object of study at the science class. In the face of such confidence I could only conceal how shaken I was at this last minute request, by hastily digging out my rod and tackle and making for the water.

Once there, my worst fears were recognised and I sat in a becalmed boat, unable to appreciate a gloriously, beautiful evening. The setting sun filtered through the crystal clear water, gilding the pebbles and fingering the sand. I prayed fervently for just a breath of wind and, if possible, some cloud to shade the golden rays.

The perpetually agitated greenshanks shrieked abuse at me from the shore and, I reflected bitterly, that this was poor thanks as, only a few days before, I had performed the delicate operation of removing a worm-baited hook, left in the shallows by some careless fisherman, from the throat of one of these fragile birds.

On a water-logged tree stump a dipper, always in evening

dress, bobbed his white shirt front up and down like a fussy head waiter, probably happy in the thought that he wasn't the only one playing the fool on the loch. Overhead a gyrating bundle of feathers spun and hovered, dived and looped and, in a static moment, revealed itself as a lively wagtail, chasing flies. He, at least, was catching something!

Suddenly I was roused to action as I felt a cool breath on my cheek, a light westerly breeze scuttled past me, trailing its coat tails along the surface of the water. My heart lifted, the fishing line sang and the artificial flies, a tempting choice of Greenwells Glory, Grouse and Claret and March Brown, lit gently among the ripples.

Little flashes of quicksilver suddenly erupted from the waters as salmon parr darted greedily towards my flies. I made to withdraw them hastily but one parr, outstripping the rest, fastened itself determinedly on the Grouse and Claret. The tiny salmon lay quite still as I dislodged the hook. I felt that its whole future lay in the palm of my hand. Would it escape all the hazards of the fresh water, the marauding pike and cannibal trout? Would it graduate successfully from a parr to a smolt, from a smolt to a grilse to become, one day, a lordly salmon; would it escape the seals and numerous other predatory denizens of the deep, not least the nets of man; would it return safely when the wild roses bloom, to its native waters to continue the propagation of its own kind? I sincerely hoped so and watched the water swallow its gleaming light.

A small cloud, no bigger than a pigeon's nest, smudged the face of the sun. This was the moment. The lures were in position again, a quick swirl in the water, the strike, the slap of the fish's tail and the triumphant screech of the reel. Softly, softly, play it gently. Keep contact all the time. But, gold as a sovereign, the fish broke the water and, with a beautiful flip, threw out the hook, and was swallowed back into the depths.

I gazed in sharp disappointment. This had happened to me before but why at a time like this?

I cast again, but my only reward was a smart little splash, a sigh from the reel and a diminutive trout which now swam vigorously around in the baling can. Modern science, I figured grimly, would surely not boggle about a matter of size, but my conscience stung severely. During the next hour I had to live with the little fish and got to know all its amphibious antics. I counted all the tiny red and blue spots that danced down its golden sides.

A fire of hatred of myself and scientists consumed me, which I could only quench by returning the trout, rejoicing, to his native element. The final flirt of its tail in the water spelt defeat; the crashing of my pillar of prestige; the end of my reign as 'the fixer'. The sun had put its light out and gone to bed, plunging the woods on the lochside into darkness and pulling a dusky coverlet over the water.

I rowed to the shore in resignation, my rod perched in the stem of the boat, making a dark pencil mark down the evening sky. The line drew aimlessly through the water and, some distance behind, the flies swam disconsolately. Almost at the boat bay, I was looking at the little tree which had miraculously sprung from a crack in a giant rock. Its leaves hung down, brushing the water, for all the world like some shadowy maiden with hair tumbled over her head, gazing into the depths.

Suddenly, with violent convulsions, my rod almost leapt from the boat and, as I caught it, the reel screamed its heart out. Wonder of wonders! A trout had seized my trailing flies just as the bow of the boat was nibbling at the pebble crusted shore.

Never was a fish handled with such care, nursed nearer and nearer, coaxed gently in the right direction to fall, a cascade of luminous colour, into the waiting net.

As the eleventh day of August dawns each year it brings to the Highlands, by train, 'plane and car, an excited flock of tweed-clad humans and they, in turn, bring the creak of new cartridge belts, the smell of gun and leather, and boxes of little brass-capped cylinders ready to explode from their polished aloofness at the tap of a gun hammer.

It brings, too, the dogs, the lunch baskets and the whisky bottles, and in the hotel lounges and bars excitement runs high and speculation is rife. Whilst, in the lodges, gunrooms and kennels, the ghillies prepare the plans of battle for tomorrow.

Who knows what tomorrow will hold?

Not I, for one, or this particular twelfth would not have found me stepping blithely through the heather with a shooting party. Bobbing and weaving around was the reason for my being there — a lively little red roan spaniel, whose owner had prevailed upon me to give the dog a turn on the moor to see how he would shape.

Ruadh was a lump of mischief in ceaseless motion, his moist brown nose ever down among the luscious scents of forest and moor. Soft brown eyes looked up trustingly, his gentle muzzle draped with velvet curtains. A perpetual, rhythmic panting rocked him gently to and fro as he watched us start for the hill.

I knew from the start I would have to keep a tight eye on this bundle of energy as soon as the shooting started and, as we walked the first 'beat', I practised putting him 'Down' to command. But Ruadh never *sat*, he flopped down obediently but wriggled with such ecstatic excitement that I was left wondering if the friction set up by the squirming of his little belly would set the heather on fire.

We soon landed right in the middle of a covey of grouse and they burst from a patch of bog myrtle in every direction. A gun barked to my left, Ruadh's ears shot to the top of his head and he sprang forward to reach the fallen bird. I turned sharply to bid him 'Sit down' when a stunning blow felled me to the heather and I wondered dully who had pole-axed me.

When things had stopped spinning and my vision cleared, I found myself on my knees. Shakily, I ran a hand round the back of my head and stared at a set of bloody fingers. Helping hands lifted me up and I was guided to a peaty water hole where my head was bathed with spaghnum moss. The cool water staunched the flow of blood and dispelled any sense of shock.

Walking in a trance I was led to the nearest transport and distantly heard the poor soul who had been on my right babbling about how he hadn't meant to fire at a bird rising between us! We bumped and jolted down the hill and eventually arrived at the doctor's house.

More mopping up by the medico,

"Umph. Ah! Well, my lad, you'll have to go to the hospital."

There I was taken in charge by a pretty nurse who 'shoo-ed' off my attendants and took me into a white room with rows and rows of gleaming instruments. The surgeon, when he arrived, treated me to a very cursory examination. The nurse, it seemed, was filling most of his eye.

"You're new here", said he, jabbing meditatively with the 'deep-freeze' needle. Somewhere behind me the husky, whispering starch of the nurse's uniform rose to an excited crackle with the answer "Yes".

"I thought I hadn't seen you before", said he again, plinking a pellet into the saucer which she held, like an offering to the gods. He was probing again, and emerged with another pellet.

"Phew! Look how they're flattened. Must have a skull like an ox."

A wave of faintness swept over me.

"Sal volatile?" She enquired almost absently. He didn't say anything but must have spared time off to nod, and I came to with the smelling salts jammed under my nose. How low, I thought, can the human race sink, to make love over what, at any moment, might become a corpse?

"What are you doing tonight?"

I was in time to hear this as I struggled up from another 'pass out' but now I was feeling a bit mellower. If these people can find love in this atmosphere of blood and ether, and if it can survive and blossom where every other germ fell flat on its face, who was I to quibble.

"There, I think that's the lot, but we'll keep hold of you for a day or two."

So the 'twelfth' went on without me and as I lay trying to forget the throbbing pain in my head my thoughts turned to a previous year and another August that I wouldn't forget.

Colin was a young gamekeeper who had two ambitions in life; to make his grouse moor the best in the Highlands and to win the hand of the lovely Morag, the head keeper's daughter.

Morag looked after the pannier ponies, whose job it was to bring out the lunch and carry back the grouse. What a picture they made! The sleek ponies with the baskets firmly strapped around their shining tummies and Morag, with her honey coloured complexion and golden hair, bringing sunshine to the moor on the cloudiest day. It was enough to turn any man's head and on this occasion it did just that.

A young gent, from the big city of London had, from the moment of his arrival, dogged Morag's every footstep. Colin had seen the intruder's advances and, with his own ears, heard him boasting of his prowess with the gun and the bag he would make at the big drive tomorrow.

Worse still, Morag was impressed and, while she flirted with the handsome city type, Colin was given the odious task of drying the oil from the interloper's guns and filling his cartridge belt and bag with ammunition in readiness for the big day. The cartridges winked knowingly at the darkness of Colin's thoughts and lit up his face with a deadly grin. Glancing furtively around to ensure he was alone, Colin set to work.

Next morning found the young city gentleman crouched in a grouse butt built of heather and turfs. Colin was there, too, with his dogs and, some distance behind, Morag with her ponies. The occupants of the butts gripped their guns in excitement as they saw, away in the distance, the tiny figures of the beaters, and the grouse rising and coming towards them with a great whirr of wings.

Flying like bullets the birds whistled overhead and the

young city lad's gun barked over and over again. But all to no avail. The speeding red grouse flew merrily on their way. It was the same at the next drive and the next.

At the end of the day Colin, whistling blithely, collected the guns and cartridge bags and set off for the big house and the gun room. Once there, he quickly opened the city gent's bag, removed the remaining cartridges, stuffed them into his pockets and made up the ammunition again from one of the boxes.

Meantime, a thoroughly bad-tempered young man was making his way back. Morosely he jerked the remaining cartridge from his belt and tossed it high in the air. Thoughtfully he caught it again and flipped the shining cylinder over in the palm of his hand. Then he searched his jacket pocket, produced a penknife and opened up the cartridge. There was no lead in it. Not a pellet!

Purposefully, the city lad strode into the now crowded gunroom. A quick glance found his gun and initialled cartridge bag. He delved inside, pushed two of the cartridges into the gun and the sharp 'snick' of the closing breech had the attention of the whole company.

"Do you wish to know why I shot no birds today?"

The young man's voice held a hysterical note as he pointed the gun to the ceiling and pulled the trigger. With a blinding flash all the lights were blown out and, in the silence that followed, the shocked occupants of the gunroom tasted the acrid fumes of cordite and listened to the 'tinkle-tinkle' of various bits and pieces being shed, at intervals, from the stricken chandelier.

At last the host, himself, emerged from under the table and, in two different languages, demanded an explanation. The young man, stuttering incoherently, was led away to receive a long lecture on the care and handling of guns.

On a drystane dyke overlooking the moor, sat Morag and Colin. The blonde head made a nest in the tweed jacket and murmured,

"Who would have though that such a nice young man would have such a horrible temper?"

And Colin, sighing innocently, replied,

"Yes, who would have thought so?"

12

Irralee always preferred having her babies at home and I can clearly recall one occasion when the local nurse was in charge. She was a likeable soul, capable and ageless, who rejoiced at every birth and promptly enlisted the little one into the huge army she called "My babies!" Always in complete command of the situation she could handle anxious fathers and young doctors with diplomatic dexterity.

At all times she was the soul of quiet confidence and would quickly size up any situation, airily assuring a distraught parent that the toy soldier little Sandy had swallowed would provide excellent roughage. But that night was the first and only time I ever saw her flustered.

Our two oil lamps burned steadily in the small hours, one upstairs, one down. I was keeping the downstairs one company when the nurse popped her head round the door and announced her light was going out. I gave her mine, which was the pressure pump variety, and received hers which flickered momentarily and went out, starved of oil. A search assured me that paraffin oil was the one thing of which we had no more.

I rummaged in the cupboards and found four candles, I lit one and kept the rest handy for reserves, which proved to be the only thing I did right. Just as my candle had produced a friendly glow I heard the nurse's anguished shout,

"Light!"

I rushed to the rescue clutching the remaining candles; to me, it felt good just to be needed for something. I was greeted by the up and down salaams of the dying lamp and as my shaking hands coaxed a flame to the third candle I realised that the nurse had just signed on another recruit for her army.

Irralee was the only one who saw the funny side and thought the whole thing a huge joke!

On another occasion, Irralee agreed to book a corner in the

homely little 'House on the Hill', especially designed for the hatching of babies, but only on the understanding that she went there at the last moment.

When Irralee eventually decided it was the moment to leave I knew there wasn't a second to spare, and cranked up the old Ford. It was a dark night as we set off, but I knew the road and reckoned we could cover the fifteen odd miles in half an hour.

About halfway there I stopped at a telephone kiosk and, after a bit of desperate fumbling for the correct money, managed to get word through that we were on our way. But the car would not start again, and the minutes ticked away. I found a small pocket torch and stabbed it around under the bonnet whilst I thought furiously. Incidentally Irralee knows a lot more about cars than I do.

I took a deep breath and climbed back into the car as casually as I could. Wondering what on earth I was going to do next I reached absently for the starter, and pulled. The engine treated us to a roar that would justify a winning goal and we were on our way again.

The feeling of relief had just seeped through me when the lights went out: I stopped the car, but this time not the engine, and snapped on the little torch. Irralee couldn't have looked more composed and said calmly,

"It doesn't look as if we're going to get there, does it?"

I always marvelled how Irralee managed to look her prettiest just before giving birth.

"Look," I said, "just you point this torch out of your window at the roadside." and we crawled and groped our way through the night.

The torch was fading and I longed desperately for more light. It came from behind, as a large, black car swept past, wailing like a banshee and drew up in front of us, flashing a 'Stop' signal. Two large figures with peaked hats appeared at my window, but before they had a chance to produce a book or speak a word, I tersely named the House on the Hill, and giving its full meaning I added "Urgent".

It was as if I had uttered a magic word. The figures spun on their heels and sprinted to their car, shouting,

"Follow us!"

Thus they conveyed us at top speed into the suburbs and other cars drew respectfully aside as the badge of office carved a way through the little township. Up the hill we swept and into the drive where the border shrubs waved us a welcome, and the cars screeched to a stop at the front door.

We got Irralee safely inside and I sat down weakly on the stone step. The 'Bobbies' sat down beside me, pushing back their peaked caps and mopping their brows. Wordlessly, I passed around my cigarettes and between puffs tried to explain about the lights going out. This jolted the men in blue.

I'm sure they had forgotten about the cause of our meeting. Without hesitation they both dived into their car and disappeared in a swirl of blue smoke, only to re-appear, seconds later, with a mechanic, who got to work on the car.

A trim little nurse smiled in the doorway.

"It's a girl." And the policemen wrung my hand as though the new little one were their own.

Next day I promised the children I would take them to see their Mummy and, of course, their baby sister. I missed Irralee's helping hand as all the things I had to do stretched out before me endlessly, and I soon found that, if I did not get going, we would be late for the evening visiting hour. So, instead of a meal, I gave the youngsters some biscuits and promised a big feast when we returned.

We arrived in good time and there was great excitement as I took the children in to see Irralee and their little sister.

On the way home everyone remembered how hungry they were, and I tried to put in the miles by painting a wonderful picture of the sumptuous meal I was going to provide. It never materialised.

Maureen was setting the table and I was fussing with the cooking pots, Valerie and Gillean were chasing each other round and round the room, when Valerie tripped and hit her face against the brick kerb of the fireplace.

After I had mopped away the blood, I found that Valerie could not close her mouth because one of her top teeth had been knocked inward. I tried to move it but the tooth remained tightly jammed, so I 'phoned the dentist and piled them all into the car again. He was just leaving for the Theatre but said he would wait for me.

In the surgery he drew me aside and asked if I could take the place of his assistant, who had long since gone home. Fortunately, it was only a 'baby' tooth and the dentist acquainted me with the apparatus and my part in the proceedings. This was to be a quick 'one, two' operation in which the patient was only out for a couple of seconds, and I was to obey his instructions in split-second timing. I stood beside the chair and smiled all the reassurance I could muster down to Valerie.

"Ready?" I flicked on a switch.

"Now!" It seemed impossible that the hand that shot out and gently placed the rubber over Valerie's face belonged to me.

"Right." I snatched the mask away again. The glint of the forceps in and out like a quick stroke of lightning. Valerie blinked and I smiled at her.

"It's all fixed," I said, and as befitted an assistant, I gave her a mouthwash and cleaned up.

We found the others being looked after by the dentist's charming wife as they tucked into huge platefuls of delicious food. Valerie joined them like a hungry hunter. The dentist beamed.

"Just look at that for a gas case", and he steered me to another room.

"We'll have to wet the baby's head. Here, have a cigar."

"But," I protested, "you were going out." A cork popped.

"Plenty of other nights."

In the face of all this kindness I couldn't speak, so I sat back gratefully and listened.

"What a day this has been. The place crammed with

people, and this afternoon, my receptionist reported that a drunk man was making a nuisance of himself in the waiting room. I went through and, with my assistant, propelled the offender outside. It took both of us, I can tell you! He was a great big, buck navvy from one of the schemes. Once outside he started to argue violently and demanded to know when he was going to get some attention and his aching tooth taken out. I told him he couldn't come here and upset all my patients and, besides, he was in no condition to have a tooth out. The big fellow reeled towards me, grabbed the lapels of my coat, stuck his hairy face into mine and said,

"Listen. Thish ish the only condition I can get a tooth out!"

"I could see it was useless to argue further, and we piloted him round the back way to the surgery. Well, after a struggle I pulled the tooth, and my white jacket suffered the most. You should have seen the mess! However, the big fellow seemed to sober with the realisation that it was all over and I could see his mouth filling. I feared for the cleanliness of my immediate apparatus, so when, through the corner of his mouth he gurgled,

'Where do I spit?' I pointed to a wash basin in the far corner, 'Over there,'"

"What," stuttered the astounded navvy, "from here?"

The dentist leaned back and laughed and I laughed too.

Our hostess was all prepared to organise beds for the night but I said,

"You have fixed our troubles, fed and entertained us, all we have to do now, is to go home. I'll never forget your kindness."

And although they are miles away, they know I never will.

Irralee's contributions toward keeping life at Croft Douglas from the ordinary path of daily routine were many and varied.

I have heard that many men have devoted time and energy towards the sole objective of producing a big bang. With no technical training whatsoever Irralee managed to produce an enormous one — with a tin of steak and kidney pie. It was placed with great care into her new electric cooker, but she forgot to remove the lid! When the cooker blew up, the blast it created, and the devastating spread of shrapnel from the inside glass door, would have made the backroom boffins turn green with envy. The grids in the oven were twisted and mangled as if by some gigantic hands. And we never did find the pie, apart from a couple of stains on the ceiling.

The man who fitted the cooker, and disbelievingly came to inspect the damage, maintains that whenever he is in need of a good laugh, he just thinks about the orbiting pie in the sky! And when we meet in the street he advances with poker face and enquires if there has been any more 'Fall-out' at Loch Tummel.

Irralee had once read somewhere that, in a far off land, people had been discovered who lived to grace the earth for a fantastic period of time, and their staple diet was honey. One of Irralee's ambitions was to gallop past the century mark, and bees were enlisted to play their part.

I soon found there was a lot more to this 'b' business than sitting around watching them clock in and out. I can also advise the kilt is no dress for working with bees! I had just completed my first attempt at fixing a frame of sections to the hive and reported back in triumph with only one sting, when everyone in the house remarked on the curious humming sound. It was finally tracked down to my kilt and a cautious peep revealed hundreds of sizzling bees in every pleat and I was bundled ignominiously outside to divest myself, and hang my tartan on the garden fence until the bees had tired of admiring the weave.

Worse was to follow. It appears that, in this district, if you keep bees you are assumed to know something about them. An elderly neighbour, who was temporarily bed-ridden, sent an S.O.S. that his bees had swarmed, and would I come. I went.

It was by far the biggest congregation of bees I had ever seen. They hung down from the apple tree like a gigantic bunch of black grapes. I confessed I had never been confronted with a situation like this before, but the old man was unimpressed. He leaned out of the bedroom window and shouted instructions.

"Put the big box underneath them. Now, hit the branch they're on as hard as you can."

I did that, too, and the black mass descended into the box like a buzz bomb, filling it to the top and overflowing in treacly waves. And the noise! If you have ever heard a boy blowing his heart out on a tissue-papered comb — just multiply that a thousand times.

"Now, turn it over!"

I turned to look disbelievingly at the old man. He was ill alright, and must be delirious. But he roared again.

"Turn it over!"

Feeling that people had received decorations for less I plunged my hands into the soft, crawling, seething multitude and upended it.

"Now, come over here." Thankfully I brushed the surplus bees from my hands, thinking it was all over. It wasn't.

The old man whipped a sheet from his bed and passed it out of the window.

"Spread that out in front of the hive over there. Take the box and shake the bees on to the sheet."

I shook them down and they exploded again. The old man was getting really excited. "Are they going into the hive?" he asked. They were, like a long winding snake.

"Catch the queen. Catch the queen."

I asked, wearily, if she was wearing a crown, but this was lost on the old man, who was rapidly coming to the boil.

"The biggest one, with the pointed tail."

They all looked the same to me, like an army on the march, but there *was* a big one with a regally tapered bottom. Quickly I emptied a matchbox and captured her, together with one of her subjects. Weakly I staggered over to the old man and firmly pressed the box into his hand and departed, praying fervently that he would soon be well!

The last I saw of our own bees was a day when some friends stopped, to show off their new car. I never found out what make of car it was, as the sky suddenly darkened and the bees rained down like a plague.

Our friends took one horror-stricken look, jumped into the car and slammed the doors. We watched in wonder as they tore up the road, with a large blanket of bees settled on their roof and the remainder trailing behind, like a plume of smoke. Mechanically, I waved farewell to the honey gatherers, without a tinge of regret.

I forget who said, 'My kingdom for a horse' but I know that Irralee would have swopped hers any day for the self-same animal and, although marriage with all its commitments had kept her out of the saddle, the passion still burned undimmed.

After the advent of our last born I thought I would give Irralee a pleasant surprise by taking her to a place where a fellow I knew was schooling horses for jumping. Irralee's pleasure at seeing the horses knew no bounds, and she begged that we should stay and watch a young horse that was about to be given a jumping lesson.

I might have known something would happen. The horse proved an unruly customer and soon demonstrated it was more than a handful for its girl rider by refusing, and throwing its rider heavily at the biggest jump. The girl was too shaken to continue, but the trainer seemed to be more concerned about the horse and kept bewailing that his best rider was on holiday and the young horse would be ruined if allowed to get away with such a blatant refusal.

Before I realised what was going on, Irralee had dumped the baby in my lap, was up on the horse and flying over the jumps. I wanted to close my eyes when they came to the big one but Irralee, with a triumphant flash of stockings and suspenders, hurled the reluctant animal over.

The children were really keen to have a pony. I tried to point out that we could graze another two heifers on the grass it would take to keep a pony. But Irralee maintained there was more to life than figuring out just how much everything ate and I wondered if, after all, my preoccupation on this subject for more years than I cared to remember had blinded me to the lighter side of life.

The light was duly flicked on by the switch of a Highland pony's tail. Luath was swift as her name implied. She was also finer in the leg than others of the Highland breed and carried herself with an extra trace of pride which, Irralee said, was the result of a light-hearted affair with an Arab somewhere down the line.

Luath quickly settled in to a strict routine at Croft Douglas. She would report at the roadside every morning just beside the showcase and, with neck stretched over the fence, would wait, ears pricked forward for the visiting cars. There she would remain all day, gorging herself with cakes, biscuits, sandwiches, fruit, chocolate and sweets of all descriptions, until I began to wonder if she remembered the taste of grass. It was when her rotund belly started to resemble a barrage balloon that we were forced to do something about it.

We shut her two fields away but, with the wings of Pegasus, she flew over the fences, fat tummy and all, and was back at the roadside before us. We were beaten, but, I thought, at least she can't read and I painted a large notice and nailed it to the fence, right at her favourite spot.

PLEASE DO NOT FEED THE PONY.

As Luath leaned expectantly over it she must have wondered what had gone wrong but, as she rubbed her chin along the top of the notice board, the answer must have come to her and she bent her head lower to cover the DO NOT far too often for coincidence to allow. We had to wait for the winter months before her girth receded.

It was in winter time that Luath sought the company of the Highland cattle and, at odd times to escape boredom, she would creep up on an unsuspecting cow and nip her. The cows took a poor view of this, but no further action. This mischief would probably have gone on unchecked but for the day Luath made a mistake and nipped the bull!

The bull wheeled round, bristling with masculinity and a thunderous 'Who did that?' expression on his face. The pony stood and watched, unconcerned, as the bull slowly eased his head down. His charge, when it came, took Luath completely by surprise and bowled her head over heels, but she was up in a flash and fled out of range.

She got up to quite a few tricks, one way and another, but she never attempted to pinch a Highlander's bottom again!

The bull who gave Luath such a striking lesson in manners was called Righ Dubh (Black King). His colouring, rare nowadays, hearkened back to the days when many of his ancestors favoured coats of jet. Righ Dubh was a regal figure, his long silken hair gleamed like the raven's wing and his magnificence was crowned with sweeping horns of polished ivory. Irralee claimed him as her own as she had been present at his birth.

The Highland cow usually leaves the fold when the birth of her calf is imminent and goes to some secluded favourite spot, which she will revisit when the call comes year after year. But, of course, where the heifer calving for the first time will retreat, is known only to her.

We always liked to keep an eye on the heifers when they came to their time and, even if I was away, a close watch was kept on them. Irralee revelled in this as it took her away from the tiresome housework. She loved to lope over the spiky hill grasses and through the heather, to listen to the quiet of the woods, to the tom-tits tapping the hazel nuts with their beaks in a non-stop effort to reach the sweetness of the kernel, and the chatter of the red squirrels as they leapt, like tongues of flame, from tree to tree, hurling all manner of abuse at any intruder.

But this particular day Irralee wasn't listening to them. She had found Riabhach (Bonny) in an exhausted heap, and immediately busied herself giving the heifer a helping hand. Between them they eventually brought her big calf into the light of day.

On my return Irralee greeted me full of enthusiasm. I

always knew when she was excited because her sentences clicked out like a typewriter gone amok, words spat out at high speed all back to front. But that night we celebrated the birth of the black bull calf.

Next day Riabhach brought her offspring along to receive the appraisal of the rest of the fold. The introduction of a new calf was quite a ceremony. All the cows gave it an individual and fastidious 'once over'. The bull allowed himself a proud parental glance, and excited young heifers crowded dotingly around, whilst the bull stirks took not the slightest notice whatsoever!

Righ Dubh gained us our first prize ticket at Oban Show and we were very proud of him and hoped, as our stock bull, he would breed plenty of black highland heifers. But in three years he only accounted for two, all the rest being coloured red or brindle.

In time, to make way for another bull, Righ Dubh found himself with a new owner. This man had a friend, Roderick, who had plagued him for years with his practical jokes. So it was with his head full of black bull that he answered the phone. It was Roderick saying that, as he would be unable to get to Perth Races he would be grateful for a spot of the right information.

"Yes," replied the new owner, "I've just got something really good, and sure to be a winner. The name is Righ Dubh."

Roderick's voice went down to an eager whisper, "Which race?"

He got the low, confident answer, "The Fair Maid's Handicap."

Roderick lost no time in burning up the wires to his bookmaker and, over a dram or two, he spread the good tidings amongst his friends. Later, an agitated Roderick phoned the new owner again.

"I've just had a call from my bookie. He says there isn't a horse of that name running."

"Not to worry", soothed the new owner, "it's a late entry,

and a dark one. Don't miss it." And Roderick parted with more cash and told more friends.

It was the overloaded bookmakers who finally tracked down, and wrung a confession, from the new owner. And Roderick, although still up to his pranks, freely admitted that the only time he was caught himself was by Righ Dubh.

13

With the forthright sincerity of four summers our youngest daughter, Shona, danced in and announced that "God is at the door." With my mind a wide open space I thanked her and made my way to the door and had to admit that the Personage outside did, in fact, bear a startling resemblance to the picture I held of the Almighty.

His silver hair framed finely sculptured features and reached down to his shoulders to merge with the flow of a majestic beard. He seemed to be engaged in intimate conversation with a tiny blue tit, which hung upside down on the languid finger of a rose bush.

If I were about to be put to the test, I thought, I would get my oar in first.

"Do you believe in spirits?" I asked.

The glowing eyes held me for a moment and a bushy eyebrow raised inquiringly. I pointed to a hole in the wall of the house.

"There is one in there." I said.

The eyebrow lowered condescendingly and he leant towards the little aperture from which a venomous hissing like some deadly snake, and a huffing and puffing as if the Devil himself were domiciled there. The stranger drew back, a smile on his face, and pointed to the tiny blue tit on the rose bush.

"His mate, she sits in there on eggs." And I had to admit this man knew what was going on in the feathered world. My eyes travelled to the smoke-blackened little tin which dangled from his hand.

"Would you like some tea?"

"Yes, thank you," his voice was gentle and cultured and I was pleased I had saved him the embarrassment of asking.

As I boiled the kettle and made up two substantial cheese sandwiches I was thankful Irralee was away on a shopping trip. How often had I teased her about her 'doorsteps to heaven' which she carved out daily for the passing 'trampies' and, sometimes, when I felt they were cutting too deeply into our budget, I would go off the deep end and tell her she was encouraging these 'milestone inspectors' to beg for food and abandon all thought of independence.

So, I had what I thought was a brilliant idea, and dragged the wooden saw-horse up to a prominent position by the door, with a log lying invitingly in its back and the saw ready for action.

"Now," I said, "if they do not volunteer, just suggest to them that if they ripped off a log or two for the fire, the kettle will boil all the quicker."

But the saw-horse waited in vain and the spiders reverently wove a shroud around it.

Somehow this man was different. He puzzled me and I thought of the story I had read to Shona, only last night, about the little girl who wouldn't share her bread with the stranger and thereafter spat out toads with her every word, and of the other little girl who. had shared and thereafter tripped gaily through life, lisping golden sovereigns. My knife passed the margarine and matched the cheese with home-made butter.

The stranger gravely thanked me for my offering, bowed and went his way. I watched him disappear round the bend of the road, floating effortlessly within his billowing robes and a red squirrel scampering along the top of the dyke to keep pace with him. Who was I to question if this man be God?

Gentleman, Sir was, I would say, an import from Ireland. He had the brogue and the blarney and his clothes were tinged with the green of the shamrock. A battered balmoral sat atop his faded purple features, which were ringed around by a flaming beard, reminding me of the land waiting to be engulfed in a heather fire. His gait was hopping, twisted, elfin-like, and one of our neighbours declared,

"He's a G- nome-ee, that one."

His method of approach was to disarm you immediately and on this occasion he leant towards me, like a stunted mountain tree which has had more than its fair share of the blast.

"Sure, I was thinkin' of you last night when I was lyin' in the roundel o' trees down the road. I was thinkin' o' the nice cup o' tea you were going to offer me, gentleman, sir."

"Indeed," I said, "you have the second sight, then?"

The flash of his eyes set his beard afire.

"It came to me as a laddie, when I saw my granny's funeral and heard the lament that Seumas, the piper, played, a full week before she was taken."

He allowed this to sink in and I could see why Gentleman, Sir never, at any time, reached starvation point. The good wives of the straths and glens, even if not fully convinced, would take no chance with Gentleman, Sir's power of vision and, indeed, would not be above trying to influence it in the right direction with an extra tasty bite or two.

"Oho! But you are the lucky one!"

"Money?" I said hopefully.

"Money!" He spat the word out contemptuously, searing and sizzling over his beard, and I knew that money to him had no connection with wealth whatever, and was just a trashy form of exchange.

"I see the grasslands rolling for miles and herds of cattle wading knee deep in lush grass. Listen to them, wrappin' their tongues around the blades. Can you not hear the soft tear of each mouthful?" He swayed as if dizzy from counting the beasts. "An' fat lambs. Oho! I never saw it better. Fields and fields of fat lambs, gentleman, sir."

The urgent chatter of the kettle lid, signifying a point long past boiling, brought me back to earth, and I reflected, as I made the tea that, in those few moments, I had been 'knocked' for at least two ham sandwiches!

I always suspected that one of our regular callers, Simple, was not so vacant as he looked. I remember his first visit and I know Irralee will never forget it!

She had gone, as usual, to the byre early one December morning and was busy coaxing the milk from our 'house' cow which, showing her true highland breeding, refused to 'let her milk down' until she had heard at least a verse of 'Cailin Mo Ruin-sa' (The Maid I Adore). A continuous performance of the song raised the tempo of the 'zizz-zizz' to full pitch as four liquid jets of milk streamed into the pail and the foaming, bubbling surface rose steadily.

It was at this point that Irralee's gaze was attracted just beyond the light of the hurricane lamp and there, in the gloom, slowly rising from the straw, was a horrible shape, resembling something between an orang-utan and a grizzly bear.

Irralee's yell would have outdone the screech of a tawny owl. The cow leapt into the air and came down with one foot in the bucket and sent it, with a quick, backward kick, full in the face of the apparition which dived, with the wail of a banshee, through the byre doorway.

Racing to the scene of the commotion, I collided heavily with the tattered monster and, travelling fast downhill, I had the best of the jump and landed with a thump on the great hairy chest. I looked down and, by the early light of dawn saw a face that only a mother could love. When the hair on the back of my neck had settled down again I found it was only Simple who had sought the warmth of the byre for the night.

He often visited us to have his blackened tea-can recharged and his hairy paw filled with whatever sustenance was going until, one day he confided to Irralee that he would like 'fresh butter and cheese' with his bread as he could never abide 'Marge and reed jeelly'. The former, he said, reminded him too much of the day he was really down on his luck and was forced to spread his piece with truck grease and the latter reminded him of a horrible road accident he had once witnessed!

I was outraged when Irralee told me of Simple's fussiness and sternly confronted him.

"Look here," I snarled, "I have a wife and four children to support and I can't afford to support you too. Have you ever tried work?"

Simple shrank back as though he had received a vicious blow and, shaking all over, he sat down weakly on the saw-horse. Beads of perspiration clung to his whiskers, glinting like drops of early morning dew and I knew that 'Work' was indeed a dirty word to Simple.

"I tried it once," he said, and his ragged frame shook at the memory.

I just couldn't help laughing and, eventually, Simple joined in but in a hollow, shocked fashion.

After that his calls were not so frequent and he never questioned the fare. I also had the sneaking feeling that he had altered the elusive and mysterious sign which trampies leave outside a country house from 'Easy meat' to 'Hard to get'.

Plausible was quite different. He, too, was a regular, and always had a very likely tale to tell of his varying misfortune.

After he had wet his throat with our tea, we would listen wearily to the woeful tale of how he had lost his good blankets. He had settled down for the night in a little ruined croft on the moor (only half the roof remained but that was better than sleeping under a threatening sky). He had been awakened in the night by a maiden's voice calling, calling, and had dashed out into the rain and followed the mocking voice far into the heather, only to find himself stranded with empty silence for a companion. Such a time he had, finding his way back to the 'clachan', only to discover that his 'good blankets' had gone.

He paused to give us the full benefit of his painful, shocked expression. We made appropriate sympathetic noises, but Plausible was steering gently to the point. We wouldn't, by any chance, have an old blanket to spare?

Irralee was always touched by Plausible's heart-rending tales and by his profuse thanks when the necessary article was produced, and on this occasion he thanked me, too, with his best poker-face, for my parting advice, "To be sure he took his blankets with him next time the maiden called him from his bed".

I was left with the thought that the blankets would go the way of all others — to be traded whenever the thirst arrived that would not be quenched by tea.

I thought I had him once when he asked if I had an old kilt to spare.

"There is no such thing as an old kilt," I informed him loftily.

But, plausible as ever, he quickly rallied and replied,

"Ach, yes. But I was meaning the ancient colours, you know."

Plausible was a piper, too, and, in the same season, he treated the tourists to his full repertoire — a scattering from various Scottish airs and his 'piece de resistance' the chorus of 'Scotland the Brave'. His income from the picked pitches when the touring coaches disgorged their loads would have brought an ashen pallor to the cheek of the Income Tax Inspector.

But Plausible was not to keep this Eldorado to himself for long. Another piper of the fraternity moved in and competition became very fierce indeed. So much so, that the newcomer blew an almighty blast that burst the bag of his pipes and they collapsed and died with a horrible drawn-out wail. And this was where plotting and planning crept stealthily into the glen.

One night there came to our door two trampies' wives. I recognised Plausible's mate. She was wildly good looking with eyes of the untamed, which trusted nothing, a torrent of

hair flowing down her neck like a golden mane which gave her the look of a filly who had never known the halter and I had the feeling that Plausible must administer a beating every week to keep her in order!

The Newcomer's wife was smaller, darker and older, with the high cheek bones of the Celt and a pair of dark, shifty 'cross my palm with silver' eyes. It was she who spoke:

"Mr. Douglas" (they always named me after the croft) "will you look after some money for us? You see," and here she assumed a coy, childish expression, "there is going to be a party tonight, and we would like the money to be safe."

As she teetered forward with a roll of notes extended towards me I realised that they had already imbibed deeply of the party spirit. I straightened out the crumpled notes and counted twenty.

"And what about these?" I pointed to the notes still clutched in her other hand.

"Oh, these," she hiccupped softly, "are for the party."

"What about the lean months ahead?" I asked sternly. "The winter will soon be here. It will be cold and hungry, and there will be no tourists then with money in their pockets. What will you do then?"

"Oh", she said, executing a tipsy pas de bas, "we never died a winter yet."

"Well," I said, "I will look after the money for you, but I must know where it has come from."

The Filly's eyes flashed and the older one of the high cheek bones drew herself up with offended dignity, saying,

"My man earned it honestly with the pipes, but he burst his bag and I want you to keep the money for her because I have just bought her man's pipes."

"And does your man know about this?" I asked the Filly, but she only tossed her mane and shied away, and I watched them drift in the direction of the nearest alcoholic supply. Like two logs in a river, they bobbed and wove their way along, gently colliding and bouncing apart, only to drift together again, as if by some magnetic quality of their liquid ballast.

Later that night the peace was rudely shattered. From the circle of silvered spruce trees where the trampies had made their camp, came a series of horrifying, blood-curdling screams. I couldn't help thinking how much the producers of modern thrillers would have cherished a recording of that hellish note!

"Murder." The word stung me into action and I had covered the first hundred yards when Irralee, with the speed of a greyhound, caught up with me.

"Don't go. Don't go. You know what they are," she gasped. "They'll only band together and turn on you. If you must go, take your gun."

I paused. This made sense and as I turned back, Irralee seized my arm.

"Listen," she said, "it's quiet now."

And it was, apart from the blessed liquid whistle of a woodcock as it flitted like a shadow over our heads.

Later that night, just after we had gone to bed I heard a sharp 'Woof, woof' from Tarra and I knew that something or somebody was moving about outside. Quietly I slipped downstairs and, in one swift movement, snapped on my torch and opened the door.

On one side of the doorstep sat the dark one with the high cheek bones, and as she looked up they were accentuated by the various shades of discolouration, forecasting the blackest of black eyes. On the other side, in a half naked heap, lay the wild Filly. Her torn clothing was pinned and tied in a vain attempt to cover the necessities. Dark red weals streaked over one bare shoulder, the other was mercifully caressed by the stained, golden mane. The Filly looked as if she had just had a long session with the toughest of horse breakers, coupled with the thrashing of her life.

I gave her a couple of aspirin, a drink of water and an old coat of Irralee's and put on the kettle. Over a cup of strong tea I got the story.

Plausible had been away all day and returned tired and hungry. He was pleasantly surprised to be surrounded by bottles of whisky and, as his thirst was always of paramount importance, he sampled the contents eagerly and drank deeply, blissfully unaware of the deal to which his pipes had been committed.

On an empty stomach Plausible was soon liquidated and only the friendly trunk of a spruce tree saved him from toppling over. As he slid down, the gnarled fingers of bark clutched at his jacket and lowered him gently to its base, and there he lay in a drunken stupor.

Everything had gone according to plan and stealthily the bagpipes, lying silent beside him, were whipped away and deposited in the Newcomer's waggon. Their pony was untethered, hitched up ready for a quick departure to pastures far away. (I never discovered if the wild Filly had tired of her mate and intended to clear out, too).

Just at that moment a tawny owl launched itself from the branches overhead, the pony threw back its head and let out a squealing neigh. Plausible rose slowly, like a creature waking from a long hibernation by the call of spring. The departing waggon came into his focus and he demanded to know what was going on. The Newcomer nervously assured him that he was going to make for the west coast, and hadn't been able to waken him to say good bye.

Plausible shook his head in an attempt to disperse the thick fog within and then, to the horror of all, announced that he would blow them a farewell! But where were his pipes? Where, indeed! After a feverish search came dark suspicion. He delved into the waggon. Everything flew! Pots, pans, blankets and there lay the pipes.

With one hand Plausible yanked the Newcomer from the waggon and with the other, felled him. His wife jumped down, screaming, to receive the next blow, but she was up like a bouncing ball shouting that the pipes had been paid for.

The Filly shrieked defiantly that she had sold the pipes and made off through the woods like a deer, with Plausible in hot pursuit, howling with rage. But he didn't howl for long, he needed every ounce of breath to catch that flowing, golden mane in front.

Weaving in and out of the trees, the Filly allowed herself a backward glance and, in doing so, tripped in a rabbit hole and came down. She was up again in a flash but the hunter was almost upon her and, wild-eyed, she started to squeal like a rabbit, which, in trying to escape the ruthless weasel, has run and dodged for so long, only to realise that, in the end, there is no escape.

The clutching hand caught her dress and ripped it off, as the wrapping leaves a chocolate box, but still she sped on, only to run into a thicket of cruel blackthorn. She turned at bay and, like the wild cat, bared her teeth and claws, but the first cut of the heavy leather belt brought her to her knees and, as it rose and fell, she screamed and screamed. This was the fearsome sound we had heard and can remember still. Mercifully, exhaustion, aided by drink, ended the torment.

So here they were to collect the money. I knew Irralee wouldn't mind about the coat and I watched the darkness swallow them up.

The Newcomer and his wife pulled out next morning and Plausible was left in undisputed possession of the best piping pitch. He and his wife must have made it up again as, a few years later, a grubby little girl, obviously on her first 'solo' came to ask for some tea and sugar. When she saucily asked for some water, too, Irralee inquired in exasperation,

"What's wrong with the burn?"

The little brows furrowed for just a moment, then she airly declared,

"It isn't working".

As we watched the little, golden pony tail bob on its way, and listened to the muffled laughter of the burn, we both thought, — how very, very plausible!

14

"Stand by, now. Stand by. Action!"

With champagne bubbles popping along my blood-stream I found my every action being recorded by the cold, critical eye of a cinemascope camera.

It all started with a telephone call saying we had been chosen as a location for making part of a technicolour film of the Highlands.

There is an old saying 'No hurry north of Dunkeld' but, obviously, the Production Manager had never heard of it. Over a cup of tea he outlined the set-up, glanced at his watch (when I though he should be consulting the calendar) and, bidding a short farewell, said,

"We'll be shooting this afternoon."

We had scarcely recovered our breath when, like the armoured spearhead of an invading army, the lumbering film units were upon us. Countless people dashed here, there and everywhere, amidst the paraphernalia that seems to be tied up with the film industry.

A couple of visiting tourists' cars were quickly wafted to the rear of the column (nothing must be allowed to spoil or interrupt the camera's view and schemes) and a tailback of cars built up in a long, winding line, some who wished to call, others who probably just wished to see what was going on.

I am quite sure the Road to the Isles hadn't seen such an ado for many a long day.

I was always under the impression that the taking of a film was a fairly straightforward operation. I couldn't have been more wrong. To me, it all seemed so frustrating. Waiting to be briefed by the Director, waiting until everything in the selected scene was 'just so', waiting until the camera crews were operational and, finally, waiting until the light was right. And to ensure you were kept properly on edge the waiting was punctuated by the 'keeper of personnel happy' checking for hysteria, the 'still' men making arrangements to 'shoot' you somewhere between 'takes' and the make-up man who went over my features with an instrument which I thought resembled a geiger counter!

The last mentioned individual put me down as 'Nil for make-up treatment' and I innocently asked if I were beyond repair.

"Oh, no", he reassured me, seriously and regretfully, "You have plenty of colour."

This was a weight off my mind, as I had no wish to undergo any exterior decorating.

The first film shots were made in an approach to Croft Douglas, and the units, like big monsters, trundled slowly forward. The camera took in Creag Mhor and the circling buzzards, then swept down to the croft, paused to admire the Royal stags' heads on the north wall, and turned the corner to peek questioningly into the show window at our display — Highland bulls and cows with their calves, red deer stags holding their antlered heads high, the hinds with fawns capering at their feet, the blackface ram, ewe and lamb herded by a watchful collie (our model of Tarra). Here, with the glint of polished ivory are the staghorn carvings and, fashioned in the beautiful colourings of the Highland cattle horn are the egg and porridge spoons, the salad servers and fruit knives, toast-racks, shoe-horns, heather vases and table lamps. Up to the hanging glass shelf and back to the stone-craft.

A little kilted laddie fishing intently, from his rod dances a gaudy fly and, rising to it, a speckled trout. Here is the Shetland sheepdog, the terriers — Scottie, Cairn, West Highland White and Skye. The red grouse and blackcock, the golden eagle with outstretched wings; a flashing silver salmon leaps to form the handle of a fisherman's tankard lured by a Blue Charm fly on one side and a Thunder and Lightning on the other.

Centrally, in pride of place, is the kilted warrior which had won us the Highland Handcraft Competition. He kneels on a hilltop rock awaiting the oncoming Redcoats. Every detail is there, the eagle plume in his bonnet, sheepskin jacket, the weave of the tartan, deerskin *cuaran* on his feet. In his right hand he clutches the basket hilted sword and on his left arm he carried the protecting targe, bearing the intricate Celtic design which, with no beginning and no end, according to legend, attracts all evil spirits catching them on this endless maze and never letting them off again.

The camera slowly backed away to take our children who, at a signal from the Director, came marching down the road and turned in to admire the showcase. At another signal Maureen picked up little Shona to give her a better look. This was the cue for the stars to appear.

"Where is the star?" I whispered to Irralee and she pointed to the kilted Adonis striding into the scene.

"I mean *the* star, the female star."

At that moment my question was answered as a beautiful girl swept forward from one of the big cars. At least, she looked beautiful from the distance, but very soon I could appreciate why this lassie had been closeted until the last moment, as the sun and wind would soon play havoc with the grease paint and the coiffure. I don't know what they pay film stars for taking periodic plunges into this clammy bog of make-up, but I hope it's plenty.

Forward to the showcase and the camera records every gesture and creeps, like a hired assassin, after the couple as they turn the corner and enter the showroom. Irralee is there to conduct them around our inside display and answer their questions. A choice is made and the male star staggers off with our biggest piece, a Highland bull, weighing between five and six pounds.

"Cut. Cut!"

He was carrying the wretched beast upside down, its thick, hairy legs sticking up in the air!

A repeat. This time the bull was his usual challenging self, right way up. The camera was silenced to close the sequence.

The Director started his briefing again. I have to take the stars on an inspection of our fold of Highland cattle and introduce them to the cows and calves (the bull, I had previously drafted away to a quiet spot, together with Kirsty, a heifer who already had to her credit the routing of at least half a dozen photographers and the destruction of more than one camera).

"Perhaps it would be a good idea if you finished this sequence by milking one of the cows."

I listened patiently to the innocent babbling and thought furiously. The only two cows that would submit to extraction by hand were due to calve and as dry as the Sahara. I knew that any of the others would kick me skyhigh if I dared to interfere with their milk bars.

I divulged this information to no-one and, when the time came, nonchalantly set my bucket under one of the faithfuls. What a wonderful, long coat she had and it draped in an all-concealing curtain! So I tickled her tum and pumped my elbows up and down as I dutifully smiled towards the 'not so all-seeing eye.' I felt the stab of deceit, but it didn't hurt much and, anyway, everybody, including the cow, was happy.

But when I thought this must be the finish I was greatly mistaken. The 'great man' buttonholed me again.

"We would like a shot of you at work tomorrow, so if you could have a piece, say within ten minutes of finishing, that will be fine."

I didn't have such a piece and was up at four thirty the next morning preparing one. By the time the outfit reported again I had an outsize bull's head almost made. The whirr of my drill cut two holes in the silence; the husky whisperings of the files, and the sweeping horns were fitted to finish the piece. There, it is done. Cut!

I never touched the head again and it remains among our souvenirs.

For many years the theatre or cinema had no place in our lives. The days had been too full, the struggle too real, there was no void to be filled with artificial drama. But now, when we do visit the silver screen I mentally slip behind the camera and say 'Hello' to the crew, to the gesticulating, shirt-sleeved

Director, to his perspiring assistant running around picking up the papers strewn around, echoing every statement the 'great man' makes and ever ready with the chair to pop under him when his legs fold up!

"Stand by!" The cups clatter down, cigarettes glow in a last desperate puff, then plunged to extinction are ground into dust.

"Action." Everything, including the human voice, went into deep freeze, only the chosen puppets moved.

15

When the last flight of swallows have winged their way south and the last curlew, with its soul-searching cry, has left for the softness of the seashore, when the wild wintry witches scream down from the north leaving the birch tree with her dress in tatters, facing the blast in stark, gleaming nakedness, when you see the ghosts of the blue hare and the ptarmigan haunting the hillsides and the red deer move down to uncover a smudge of moss, a spike of grass or a sprig of frozen heather, it is time to see that the house cow is snug in the byre and to check on the stores of turnip and hay, time to see that the meal barrel and flour bin are full and to look again at the wood shed, time to sit at the fire and watch the logs crackling and glowing.

But starving deer were outside, an anxious, jostling herd, feverishly hunting for food. The hated man smell filled their nostrils. They should be afraid and run! But starvation holds a higher command than fear. They must eat now or die and just a bare mile away to the west of us, on a croft sitting higher on the hill, the deer have discovered something. Rows and rows of ungathered turnips, and they devoured them in ravenous, rasping bites.

Almost as if he heard them, young Lachie looked up from his supper plate.

"Father," he said, "the deer will be eating that break of turnips we didn't get in."

His father looked across from his seat by the fire, removed his pipe and said slowly,

"Well, boy, there is nothing we can do about it tonight."

But the blood coursed young and strong in Lachie's veins. He jumped up impatiently and reached for the rifle above the fireplace.

"Oh, yes, there is," he said. "And I'm the one to do it,"

Outside in the darkness Lachie realised he could not tackle this job alone, so he skirted the turnip field and quickly made his way down to the little hotel at the foot of the hill where the host and his wife, Hector the post, and myself were discussing arrangements for a forthcoming ceilidh. When Lachie opened the door, he stood blinking as the beam of light beat at his eyes.

"Will anyone come with me and get some of the stags that are eating our turnips?"

"Oh, Lachie," I said, "Any other night, but it's Sunday, the day that everything should have to itself. I remember, when I was just a lad, there was a man who dearly loved a shot, a day hardly went past when he wasn't out chasing something or other.

"One Sunday he got up early to go after rabbits. It was a nice, sunny day and the bunnies were out having their breakfast. But the man had to negotiate a wire fence to get within shooting range and as he crawled underneath, the bottom wire pulled back the hammer of the gun he hugged to his side, and that was where they found him."

I turned to Lachie and carefully handed him each word.

"That man was buried unmourned by the entire community because he was out shooting on a Sunday."

But Lachie spurned the message behind the tale with a shuffle of his feet. He enlisted the support of the host's son and, with the bravado of youth, they both set out, closing the door on my final words,

"No good will come of it. Not on a Sunday."

Much later that night I was on the point of bidding my host farewell when his son, pale of face and panting for breath, burst through the doorway, gasping:

"Lachie's been hurt."

Lachie and the boy had set out for the turnip field and, by the light of a tipsily balanced new moon, had seen the deer, around thirty or forty shadowy shapes which, by now, must have been fully aware of the strong-smelling human approach. But empty bellies cried to be filled and the deer lowered their heads again and stuffed the turnips back.

On instruction from Lachie, the boy had moved quickly round to where the deer would break for the moor and when Lachie moved forward to them the boy's rifle spat and the bullets whined. The herd, with one accord, bolted towards the high fence and flew at it like long, shadowy birds.

The boy at the fence, unnerved by this ghostly, thundering cascade, saw the wildly plunging shapes gather themselves and launch out gracefully in extended flight over the high wires. He fired wildly and desparately at the last of them, but now they had gone. All but one, a ten-pointeed stag, momentarily sickened by the bullet which had torn its stomach.

Rushing forward in triumph, the boy was stopped in his tracks by a warning shout from Lachie and the sight of the big stag now up on his feet. With an aggressive sweep of its antlers the wounded beast defied any approach and, knowing it could not now jump the big fence, it turned and saw the gate which Lachie and the boy had left open.

Only one thing barred its way, Lachie. He had foreseen the stag's next move and had got there first. Lachie took a cool and steady aim at the advancing beast but, just at the moment when the curling finger squeezed the trigger, the antlered

head was lowered in a desperate charge and the bullet winged harmlessly into the night.

With no chance to shoot again, Lachie threw aside his rifle and grabbed the antlers, one in each hand! The sharp tines tore his hands but he held on and he and the stag were locked together in a fearsome fight. Lachie was fortunate. The frozen snow gave his tackety boots a good firm hold. Not so the deer, whose striving clits slipped and slithered furiously in a desperate attempt to secure a grip. Lachie nearly paid very dearly for daring to take on the stricken stag in hand to hand combat.

As it was, Lachie was in a sore plight. His strength was failing but he daren't let go or the animal would have him at its mercy. It was then he saw the boy approaching.

"Shoot. Shoot!" he gasped and, with a valiant pull on the antlers, turned the deer's side towards the pointing rifle. There was a sharp crack and the stag collapsed in a limp heap on top of its adversary.

At first sight, we thought Lachie was done for, too, but he didn't look half so bad when the stag's blood was washed off and there was only his to contend with.

I was deeply thankful that Lachie's injuries were not serious, and not only for Lachie's sake! I knew full well that everyone in the present company had no doubt at all that, with my rambling predictions, I had largely brought about the whole situation.

So it was with great measure of relief that I noticed the door open again to a good figure of a man, a piper from Blair Atholl. In no time at all he was acquainted with the happenings of the evening.

"Well now," said the piper, downing a dram and calling for another. "It was about time that you Loch Tummel folk came up with something to match all those tales about the wild men of Rannoch," and the piper paused to sip his second dram fastidiously, in marked contrast to the speedy dispatch of the first.

"Now," he continued, "I remember my father telling me

that Strathtummel used to boast of having he wildest man of all. He was a man of no great stature, could never rise above five and half feet in his heavy brogues, but was as broad as he was long with legs as stout as bog oaks, a chest like the front end of the Ballachulish ferry. His name was Calum Og."

The piper, almost casually, revisited his glass, then suddenly bobbed out of it again saying,

"It was when the cows in Strathtummel were all bawling unashamedly, and in vain, for a bull. But the local bull was dead, and the crofters had a meeting to arrange the purchase of another communal bull. Times were hard in those days. A severe winter with hay and potatoes at starvation level had emptied larders and pockets, and the most the good men could raise between them was a handful of silver, barely enough, as one put it, to 'Buy the bellow.'

"This, you understand, all took place long before a cow's mating call could be relayed by telephone to bring a man in a fast car who peddles a variety of sires neatly packed into little glass tubes. So there was no question of solving the problem this way and they all looked pretty glum, when one man spoke up.

"He said he had been visiting Blair Atholl the day before and had seen a big Highland bull all alone and very much out of work, grazing in the Castle grounds. This announcement provoked an animated discussion, and it was finally agreed that someone should be chosen to go and ask for a loan of the bull.

"But who would have the right tongue to ask for the animal and the muscle to bring it over? The choice was whittled down by vote, to one who was thoughtfully engaged in tracing his name on the floor with the foremost tacket of his boot — Calum Og.

"Next morning Calum set off over the hill and across the moor to Blair Atholl. There, he rapped smartly on the iron-studded door with his sgian dubh and the girl who answered him ran, at his bidding, to fetch the Factor. Calum swept off his bonnet.

"'Our bull at Strathtummel is dead, and we wish to ask for the loan of yours.'"

"'Yes, yes, certainly, my man', said the Factor. 'The bull is over there in the park, but he is a big fellow with a nasty turn of temper. How do you propose to get him over to Tummelside?'"

"Calum smiled a slow smile and unwound a rope halter from his waist. The Factor watched amazed, as Calum slipped the halter on to the surprised bull and towed him away.

"They were well over the hill and on to the moor approaching Loch Bhac when the bull recovered from the shock and launched a ton of aggravation into the small of his tormentor's back. Calum Og picked himself out of a patch of bog myrtle and addressed the bull.

"'Well, now. It's pleased I am to see that you are breathing and able to do something for yourself. Now, maybe, you will come the rest of the way without dragging your feet', " and he picked up the end of the halter and set forth again.

"But they had just gone a few yards when the bull dug the point of his left horn deeply into Calum's ribs. The lad spun round with a gasp and gave the bull a hefty punch in the ribs, whereupon the bull retaliated by tossing Calum neatly over his shoulder. They had a real set-to and the black-headed gulls rose from the loch, adding to the uproar by wheeling and squealing continuously over the scene of battle.

"For a long time they fought, bull and man, until Calum got a cross hold on the bull's horns, and, with an almighty heave and a roar that exploded the cloud of gulls into screaming fragments, he threw the bull. But, oh, shades of purple heather! In so doing, he broke the bull's neck and it collapsed into a peat bog with a last pathetic bellow.

'Bo-aa-hah-hah, bo-aah.'

Calum stood over the body, his chest heaving like a boat in a storm.

'Bo-aa-hah-hah yourself,' he said. 'It wass yoo who started it.'

"Oho, ho," chuckled the piper. "He was a *wild* man, was Calum Og."

16

We worked steadily during the winter evenings, I designing and making the models, whilst Irralee did the painting and titivating. And, as we worked, all manner of topics were discussed.

One evening, a week before Christmas, I happened to mention that I had read somewhere that, as one passed the thirtieth milestone the ability to absorb, retain and say a verse or two of poetry became more difficult. Irralee thought the writer maybe had a point as the brain, if not used, could become lazy, but I strongly opposed this view and a heated discussion was soon in progress.

I wasn't doing too well and was deciding to retire from the fray, when my eye caught an illustrated supplement to one of the newspapers. I reached out and found it was Robert Burns' 'Tam o' Shanter'. Waving it aloft, I said,

"Do you see this? I could have this off by heart in a week."

Irralee's reply was, "We shall see."

Why, I thought, had I not kept quiet and surrendered peacefully. Now I would have to spend a lot of precious time reading, digesting and committing to memory something which, I was sure, wouldn't interest me in the slightest. I could hear accursed vanity laughing its head off!

I had not perused Burns beyond the 'Wee, modest, crimson-tipped flower' and 'Wee, sleekit, cowrin', tim'rous beastie' of early schooldays, but 'Tam o' Shanter' intrigued me immediately. I felt the power of it overcome me; it was strong meat that gripped my insides and the weaving of the tale made a loom of my backbone.

To memorise this masterpiece was unnecessary, it had been written with something more than a red hot poker, and every line burned in my mind to stay.

One night, after we had gone to bed, Irralee teasingly asked me how 'Tam' was coming along and I found relief in letting it pour out of me. I didn't get far, as Irralee dived out of bed and refused to return until I desisted. I felt satisfied I had put the message across.

In a confiding moment at a New Year party, I was joking with some friends about my introduction to 'Tam' and during a lull in the proceedings they persuaded me to try it out. I was doing fine, or so I thought, when a high pitched voice cut right through the ghoulish party at the Old Alloway Kirk.

"I hate Burns."

The scream mowed down the dancing witches more effectively than a nest of machine guns and the whole scene vanished as if it had never existed. I swore in those moments that never again would I even wear a tam-o-shanter.

But Burns's birthday came around and, the day before, a telephone call inviting me to recite at a local function.

"And," the feminine voice continued sweetly, "we will just get you to address the haggis, too. Thank you so much".

Ching. She was off the line before I had time to protest that I wasn't even on speaking terms with a haggis.

Irralee hunted the house, in vain, for a book on Burns and eventually borrowed one from a neighbour. She also returned with the information that there was a Burns' Supper in Pitlochry that night and thought I should go and see how things were done.

So there I was at my first Burns' Supper. If it had not been for my own trial on the following night I would really have enjoyed it. But, as it was, I tried to absorb everything that was going on — the Chairman's welcome, the piping in and address to the haggis, the speeches, toasts, the songs and the elocution.

I arrived on time next evening for my personal initiation feeling that, with a bit of luck, I might just manage it. But as I witnessed the arrival of the guests my heart sank lower and lower. They would expect nothing but the best.

Piloted to a seat at the top table beside the host, I glanced furtively at the long arm of people sweeping down to my left, of cocked-up napkins, faces and decorous chatter; to my right, the same again and, coming towards me, buckling a bit at the knees, but egged on by the skirl of the pipes, came a little Swiss maid who, with a sigh of triumph and relief, deposited her load in front of me.

It was the biggest haggis I had ever seen, as plump as a pumpkin. I rose to face its challenge.

"Great chieftain o' the puddin' race." My thoughts raced ahead. Where was the knife? One was provided at last night's 'do', but it was a lady who had done the honours and, of course, no lady would carry a knife in her garter. That was it! I was expected to use my sgian dhubh.

My hand slipped down and drew the blade just in time for the cue of the verse. I struck one end of the haggis a weighty stab as I expected a haggis of that size to have the hide of an elephant, but either it wasn't as thick as I had estimated, or my blade was a deal sharper than I had imagined.

It unzipped one side its full length as cleanly and swiftly as a dorsal fin cuts the water and a cloud of steam belched up and enveloped me. This went down well and I must have looked like some mad dervish as I danced about in the billowing puffs and cut off the 'legs, an airms, an' heids.'.

Flushed with success and the smoking 'entrails' of the haggis, I made a passionate appeal to the ceiling that Scotland should always be provided with such a dish and, as my eye swept downwards to embrace my victim with the last line I saw the gleaming, untouched bulge of the pumpkin.

With a quick and impulsive aim I threw my sgian dubh into it and watched it bury itself to the haft. I could hear the snarling grate of the point as it struck at the china of the ashet and saw my host, with a twinkle in his eye, take a quick peep under the table to see if the steel blade had, indeed, penetrated the table, too.

With a pretence of great strength he pulled out the sgian dhubh, placed it on a plate beside me and proceeded to dish out the haggis, while I wondered how I was going to wipe the blade before returning it to its sheath. For a shameful moment I eyed the mealy-coloured curtain which draped down the back of my chair, but it drew itself together and cringed away. On turning round again I found that the weapon in question had vanished!

The little Swiss maid, who had interpreted my searching glances, hurried to my side and, in a confidential whisper, assured me that she would return my 'daigger' when it had been cleaned in the kitchen.

As I worked my way through my own mound of haggis I daren't even think of 'Tam o' Shanter' but, in no time at all, or so it seemed, I was called to my feet.

How on earth does it begin? I played for time by measuring safe distance, in an exaggerated manner, to avoid breaking anything or accidentally felling a neighbour. Some kind soul read my thoughts and put out the main light leaving the table softly aglow and, in the shadow beyond, the scene was revealed to me.

Now, into the Inn. The tang of spirits eats its way through the billowing tobacco smoke and here, at a table, by a roaring fire, sits Tam and, amid the clatter of tongues and songs, his story-telling bosom friend, Soutar Johnny.

This is the meat that Tom is hungry for, the drink is at his elbow. I feel the warm glow of every sup, feel it strike at the binding shackles of daily toil. I see care topple from Tam's shoulder and fall 'plop' into the nearest foaming tankard to drown, ignominious and unmourned. With Tam I am free and triumphant, caring nought for the howling storm outside, forgotten the long, lonely road home; forgotten, too, the wife who waits there, her rocking chair beating out every second and hotting up the rhythm of her wrath.

I pluck the poppy of pleasure, only to watch the petals fall to the ground. I see the dainty snowflakes kiss the water and die. I trace the lovely rainbow in the sky and obliterate it with a storm cloud. Like hatching butterflies, the golden moments wing their way dizzily. But Time, inevitable and invincible, drives Tam into the saddle of his fleet grey mare, and he is off into the night, the wind shrieking in his ears, stifling his breath and tearing at his clothing. The lashing, blinding rain forces him to bow his head.

But the chill doesn't penetrate and cannot really grapple with the warmth of the drams within and he croons an old Scots ballad to the drumming of Meg's hoofbeats. Past the dyke where the shepherd fell exhausted and was smothered in a snowstorm; past the big rock where old Charlie tipsily broke his neck; through the clutching whins that shielded the lifeless child; past the thorn tree that showed the way out to Mungo's mother, the drooping branch an etching against the sky, the dangling legs and wrinkled stocking.

Before us, the waters of the Doon river roar in spate and, to the left, the old Alloway Kirk, strangely lit and weirdly noisy. Bold as brass Tam turns his mare and urges the unwilling beast towards it.

What a scene! The Kirk is packed to suffocation with witches and evil spirits, and how they madly dance and twirl, inspired on by no less a personage than the Devil himself, perched on a window sill playing the pipes. The sight of the twisting, flapping, hideous creatures, the acrid smell of sweat and brimstone would set the strongest stomach on a reel of its own and there, in the centre, are the grisly exhibits.

I shiver over the bloodstained weapons, weep for the tiny, unchristened babies; choke over the strangler's garter; gasp for the thief wearing the hangman's rope; shrink from the terrible knife that had slid across the old man's throat after it had slain his son, the grey hairs still stuck to the haft. And more. Horrible!

I bury my face in my hands. It is too much. I look up again and see a young lady's face. Is she here, or there? I don't know. I am too busy peering into each of the open coffins. The shrouded occupants have the cold, magnetic spell of the snake. What wizardry has placed a tiny light into each uplifted hand?

The tempo of the pipes rises to a deafening crescendo that shakes the very rafters. The witches cast off their clinging, steaming, sweaty rags and whirl faster and faster and there, in the centre of this crazy whirlpool, a maiden dances a wild, magnificent solo. A new recruit only that night, she had joined the ranks of the witches, her fresh, young, voluptuous body as yet unwithered and, as she leaps and flings, her short little gown strives to cover the dancing limbs.

Tam applauds and roars his approval. In that instant the inmates of the coffins douse their lights and we are plunged into darkness. The screaming, furious witches pour out at Tam, and he puts 'the heels' to Meg and flies for his life. After him, in full cry, screech the hellish mob.

"Oh, Tam, they'll have you! Feverishly I urge him on, faster, faster. Make for the bridge, it is your only chance. They can't cross running water!"

"Faster, faster!" I lash the mare with every word, but the comely maid outstrips them all in pursuit and gains on Tam with gigantic bounds. Her white thighs gleam as she takes a flying leap, her bare feet claw a footing on the mare's rump. She screams with triumph as she clutches the flowing tail. But, in one colossal bound Meg reaches the water.

I can smell the horsey sweat, feel the heaving flanks, and am soaked by her lather. Meg has Tam safe, but I sob over the loss of her beautiful grey tail. I pause for breath and rally my last reserves.

The faces of the audience came back into a hazy focus, the doctors, the dentists, lairds, lawyers and businessmen, sitting like a class of small boys. I marvel at the power of this moment as I gathered them together and dealt out the last warning lines,

"Remember, when you reach for the brimming glass; remember, when you gaze on hot-blooded excitement, scantily clothed, remember the faithful grey mare."

It was over. I flopped down exhausted and the next few minutes escaped me. They had tip-toed silently away. As one who has thirsted in the desert I reached for the sparkling glass, in the fervent hope that it was not just a tantalising mirage. It felt like the cooling sip from a mountain burn and, with the bubbles, I surfaced to normality and the pleasant murmur of conversation.

17

Today Angus had received from the hands of Hector, the post, a brown paper parcel containing a loaf of bread. A neat piece of surgery produced, from its inside, a bottle of 'Mountain Dew'. It was a present from a friend in the Islands, one of the last in 'the business.'

With infinite care, Angus tilted the bottle and watched the crystal cascade plunge eagerly into his glass and climb with a soft, intimate gurgle, to the top. Then he raised the glass, balanced delicately between finger and thumb, to eye-level and gazed into it intently. From its stance on the kitchen dresser the soft, yellow light of the paraffin lamp burned through from the other side, flanked by the shining arc of the old clock's pendulum and the warm glow of the peat fire.

Like a cockerel at the drinking bowl, Angus sipped each drop with a deep satisfaction, then paused to fill his pipe. This was an elaborate operation involving much excavation with a knife, the meticulous shredding of the tobacco between the heel of one hand and the palm of the other, the careful packing and tamping down for the final sacrifice. A match flickered and the smoke billowed out to meet a loud knocking at the door.

"Come away in," shouted Angus and blew another cloud of smoke, which recoiled violently as the door opened admitting two of the glen shepherds, their steps light with the spring of inebriation.

"Oho, Angus," said the tall one, "We are on our way from the sale."

"Yes," said the little one, "and we thought we'd call and have a ceilidh with you."

"Well, look at that now," welcomed Angus "Pull yourselves a chair."

Then, in a conspiritorial tone,

"I have a real treat for you, boys. A drop of the real stuff."

"Slainte!" Three heads rolled back in unison and returned with a chorus of approving 'aahs.' The small shepherd waved his hand apologetically at his bottle.

"I'm telling you this will be only mouthwash now."

Another glass, then another and the tongues began to wag.

"We sold the 'Leaper' today." The tall shepherd made the pronouncement with the air of a major achievement and, by way of explanation, he added,

"That's what we named one of our stirks. His mother was the dun cow that always grazed at the top of the hill, and I'm certain sure she got too friendly with the stags because her calf, when it came, was the wildest thing that ever leapt the crags of the hill. Twice we tried to get it down for the market and it ran the insides out of us, and the third time, with a bit of extra help, we actually got it into the loading pen and it cleared the top bar like a bird."

"Oho," chuckled Angus. "The mother had been with the stags all right. Go on, go on."

"Well," continued the tall one straightening up the small shepherd with a dig of his elbow. "It was Jamie here who had the grand idea. There was a bunch of students camping at the top of the glen and he suggested that we should get the youths to give us a hand. I can tell you, we were getting desperate to sell the beast before it grew antlers! So we made our way to the camp and the lads, about forty of them, were in the middle of a meal. 'Oho boys,' I said, 'How would you like a haunch of venison to go with those beans?' I tell you I never saw so many plates of beans deserted so quickly. Well, I remembered reading how those natives caught the lions by making a human ring round them and that's what we did with the Leaper. We surrounded him and eased him down the hill, and each time he tried to break the circle the lad at that point would shake his stick or growl, or make a face. It was slow work and those beans must have got awfully cold, but we eventually got the stirk to the box trailer and, making a small gap in the circle there was only one way for him to jump. Into the box! He was caged now and we shut the door tightly, I can tell you."

Angus knew there was more to the tale than this.

"And the market, What happened at the market?"

But the tall shepherd found the need to pause for another dram before he continued.

"Well, we got to the market all right, but as soon as the box trailer was opened the stirk left it like a bolting hare and started to leap the pens in real Grand National style. I thought to myself, that in two or three minutes he'll have cleared the lot and be out of the county. But just then he landed in a pen of big bullocks and was jammed, fair and square, between their fat sides.

"The owner of the bullocks strode forward to help me out but I dashed up and persuaded him to leave things as they were until the sale started, and that's the way the stirk got up the alley and into the sale ring — wedged in a pack of fat bullocks.

"The auctioneer knocked him down to a buyer from the South, but the stirk spotted the open door before the bullocks and he was through it, bullet fashion, and leap, leap, leaping every pen and fence that came his way. This was the moment we nipped smartly round to the Office to collect our money and made for home.

"We stopped at the nearest Inn and had a dram to steady our nerves, but it took four or five, I can tell you. Then a fellow came in and says in a voice for all to hear,

" 'I never saw the like. A Sassenach chasing a beast all over the town and, when I left, it had been in every garden in Aberfeldy.'

"In the excited babble that followed Jamie and I finished our drinks and slipped quietly away."

Angus saved his pent up roar for this moment and the three of them rocked and rolled with laughter.

"Oho," said Angus, wiping away a tear. "The best I've heard for a long time. Now we'll have another dram and then I'll show you a ram, the likes you've never seen before."

The three of them staggered to a shed outside.

"There," said Angus, throwing open the door. "What do you think of him?"

It was dark inside, so Angus sparked a match. "There, isn't that the finest head that ever was?"

"Catch hold of him," said little Jamie, who rather fancied himself as a judge of Blackface rams.

128

Angus, trying to oblige, tottered forward with outstretched arms, but the ram eluded him and left Angus rolling about in the straw. The shepherds laughed aloud.

"Well, well," they said to each other, "which one is the beast?" Angus arose not in the best of tempers and was immediately aggravated further by Jamie's next remark.

"I think the bodach's forgotten what a sheep looks like."

"Och," roared Angus, "I knew a sheep before you were lambed yourself," and reached out for the little man to hammer home his point. But Jamie was too quick and danced away and round about, tapping Angus' backside with his boot just to keep him going, and it did, too.

Like a badger baited by a terrier Angus clawed the air to get at his tormentor. He had been a wrestler in his day and, at the moment, sought with all his might to embrace the little shepherd, who slipped, and fell into the eager arms. Angus, with Jamie clutched tightly to his breast, swayed and fell forward.

"Where are you? Where are you? Jamie!" gasped Angus. But, Jamie, lying underneath, had parted with every ounce of wind and was unable to reply. The tall shepherd, whose merriment had taken him almost to the point of collapse, helped Angus to his feet and between them they dragged the limp little form back to the house.

Angus was greatly disturbed at Jamie's condition but the tall one, between gusts of laughter, said,

"Ach, there's nothing wrong with him that a good 'hooker' won't put right."

And so it proved. Another round of drams brought the little shepherd back into the picture and good spirits were restored.

Angus began to sing, the shepherds backed up with the chorus and in the middle of a merry rendering the door flew open and in flounced Angus' very small, but very capable wife. She opened fire right away.

"Look at the mess. I can't even go away for the day. The fire's out, the room's in a 'boorach' and reeking of whisky."

The tall shepherd rose respectfully, Jamie managed the half-open, half-shut jack-knife position, but Angus brushed away his 'better-half's' tirade, midge fashion. This so incensed the good lady that she darted to the table, grabbed the two bottles of whisky and upended them over the sink.

Angus looked on, horror stricken. Then roaring like a Highland bull, he heaved his bulk out of the big chair and, seizing his wife round the waist, held her airborne for a moment before deftly hanging her by the coat collar on the hook behind the door.

"There," he croaked, "just you cool off in the skin you got hot in," and the good lady arched and fluffed like a treed wild cat.

Angus reeled over to the sink, rubbed his hands across his eyes to dispel the nightmare, and gazed mournfully at the plughole. There was a soft belch from the waste pipe, and a bubble popped up just below the grating.

"Quick, boys, there's a choke, get me a bowl!" and, like a man possessed, Angus dived below the sink, undid the screw, and the contents of the trap splurged into the bowl. Flushed with triumph he emerged with the salvaged whisky and, with the generosity of success, lifted his little wife down from behind the door.

"Now Flora," he said gently, "The boys really called because you put on the best table in the glen," giving her a playful pat on the bottom which propelled her through to the kitchen.

And there the good lady reflected, that after all, they were real men, and as she opened the door of the food cupboard and drew out a huge game pie, she knew how it was going to be appreciated. And wasn't hers the hand behind it?

In the room the shepherds gazed dubiously at the murky liquid in their glasses.

"Ach, well," said Angus. "It was a good ceilidh we had boys. Slainte."

And he tipped back his glass, drained it, and spat the tea leaves into the fire.

18

In October, when the earth is drawing the sap back to her bosom to conserve it for yet another year, the countryside dresses up, not in mourning for the dying year, but to stage a final carnival of glorious colour. This is the time to see the straths and glens at their very best, when the early morning frosts put a tinsel on the tints and turn the air to wine.

This, too, is the time to hear the big stags roaring as they stride through the heather and birch with majestic step, and assert their rights. No longer are the days spent in furtive feeding and in constant flight from man.

The Monarchs of the Glen hold their antlered heads high, and blood storms through their veins as they seek out the hinds and do fierce battle for their favours. Don't cross his path. Fear of man is, for the moment, forgotten and, indeed, if you have never felt your scalp tingle, or the hairs at the nape of your neck curl tightly, just get to within a few hundred yards of a challenging stag, particularly at dusk.

It was at a white hare shoot, on the south side of the loch, that I first met a big stag, face to face. These hare shoots were an annual occasion organised by the sheep farmers, who maintained that the large number of hares on their hills tainted the grazing for the black-faced sheep. I must confess, this seemed to me rather a twisted viewpoint as, in my opinion, nothing taints the ground more than sheep — but probably my views are through the jaundiced eyes of a cattleman! However, I joined this particular shoot to find out exactly what went on, and as a chance to get to know the hills on the other side of the loch.

We met on the shoulder of Schiehallion on a cold, crisp morning and, as I didn't relish the idea of shivering behind some dyke or distant butt, I elected to be with the party who were to do most of the walking and drive the hares into the hidden guns. At the same time we were supposed to pick off any that fled in the wrong direction.

Spreading out in a long line we swept forward, striding through the bog myrtle, which soon gave way to heather, where disturbing the red grouse, they whirred away like a warm-winged mahogany, shouting 'Go back, go back.' But we didn't. And as we climbed higher and higher, the snow, just a dusting at first, became deeper and deeper, making heavy going indeed.

Soon the hare were exploding out of the snow in front of us and flitting away like ghostly wraiths. I wondered why nature had painted the eartips black. Had she sacrificed complete camouflage for a touch of beauty? It seemed so strange that the blue summer coat of the hare, a perfect blend for the heather, should so miraculously turn to white when the snows came, all but the tell-tale black tips. Was that what the golden eagle saw to send him plummeting down for his favourite dish? I don't know. But I do know that, in this world of white, the flying tips attracted the beads of the gunsights.

For myself, I found the furry, flitting forms that sent up little powdery spurts of snow as they darted away, wildly beautiful and faerylike, and wished good fortune to those that went forward. The ones that went back I had great difficulty in seeing!

But as drive succeeded drive and we climbed higher and higher, reaching for the heights of Creag-an-loch and Faragon, and to the very cloud itself, where I found I had no need for any form of pretence about visibility and the hares.

An all-enfolding mist descended like a wet, woolly blanket, and I found myself wandering in a little, quiet circular world of my own. I could see no one, and stopped to listen for the crunch of neighbourly footsteps, then even for the sound of a shot. But there was nothing. Not a whisper and the icy cold reached right through me. I stamped to keep the circulation going and hoped that I wouldn't end up as just another tale of someone lost in the hills.

The mist cleared a little and I could now see for about

thirty yards. A hare started in front of me, but only bounded a little way, then sat up and looked back, and I wondered if this one had been making a tally of all the lives I had spared and was now beckoning me to the path I must take. But it loped off out of sight and I mentally burnt all faery tales and felt slightly warmer for it.

In the next moment — disaster! The surface that had safely taken the dancing hare had collapsed under my weight and I plunged through the icy crust, down into the soft core of a bog. It was cold. Oh, so cold, and I froze up to my armpits! With my gun spread out before me I struggled madly to be free of the clammy, clutching bog and, inch by inch, tried to lever myself out.

I paused for breath and, looking up, saw a shadowy form come out of the mist. All was well, this would be one of the party. But it wasn't. It was a great big stag, stepping forward with the grace of a thoroughbred, and towering over me. He had the flanks and quarters of a hill pony, the chest and mane of a lion, and how lightly and regally he carried those massive antlers. In a daze I counted the antler points, twelve, a royal stag!

For a long, long moment he studied me then, with a contemptuous blow down his nostrils as if I were only a tattered corpse that some wild cat had finished with, the big stag turned round, as though on well-oiled wheels, and disappeared as quietly as he had come. I hadn't dared to move when he was looking me over, and now, frozen to the bone, I fought to finally pull myself out of the bog.

Floundering through the snow, I wondered how long I could keep going; the cruel, clawing winds of the summit had numbed me completely down one side. Then I saw a dark patch on the snow, a cavern that bid me share its shelter. Scrambling, I fell headlong into it, right at the feet of a man.

Another human being! I tried to talk, but my teeth rattled in my head like a mouthful of glass beads. My companion pressed a bottle upon me. I drank and drank. I didn't feel warm or cold, and I can't remember the taste, but its effects were immediate. The ice in my veins thawed out, a warm glow kindled within me and spread to every fibre. I sat down with my back to the rock and closed my eyes, revelling in the ecstasy of the moment.

"Nothing like a drop of the barley," my benefactor assured me, and went on to tell me that he, too, had lost the main party and was waiting for the mist to lift. Scarcely had we finished a companionable cigarette than the surrounding clouds rolled up, like a massive stage curtain and revealed the countryside at our feet. And there, far below, lay the blue waters of Loch Tummel, bathed in sunshine.

It was just like starting life all over again, and as we slipped from our shelter two winged snowballs whistled at express speed over our heads — ptarmigan. Like the mountain hares, these birds change to white with the first cold, snowy blast of winter. The ptarmigan prefer to stay on the lonely mountain tops, kindred spirits with the hares in a world of their own, far removed from the haunts of Man.

We soon contacted the main party and a count was taken to make sure no-one was still missing, and off we set on yet another drive.

I recognised the young fellow on my right as the guest of one of the farmers on holiday from Glasgow. This lad had set a strong pace in the morning and he was still stepping it out. I, for my part, was feeling very tired and the muscles on my legs were cramping viciously.

Another mile. And yet another. Will he never slow down? I wondered if the others were feeling as I did. But no-one gave the 'Go slow' or 'Stop for a rest' signal. I felt that time was running out for me, and what degradation to bow the knee!

But Fate, for me at least, was kind. The tall lad from Glasgow stumbled, and hung for a moment as a tree under the final stroke of the woodman's axe. Crash! He fell full length, to a soft bed of snow-blanketed heather. What a relief! I was not alone with this unkind thought as everyone flopped down, only too thankful to rest, while the young lad recovered from overrunning the 'engine'. And as I sat, I thought of Dougal and the day he fought his endurance duel.

Dougal was a stalker and, as his title suggests, his main job was to take the laird's guests out to the hill, and with skilful manoeuvring through the rocks and heather, put them in a good position for a shot at a suitable stag. The rest was up to them.

Dougal was not a big man. The loss of his thatch prematurely, aged him deceptively, and his spare, bony frame carried only the minimum of flesh. But, to all who knew him, Dougal was a force to be reckoned with. His muscles were forged on the mountain tops and bound together with sinews tougher than the heather and beyond all breaking points.

He could lope for miles on the hill with a pair of lungs that operated as smoothly as the blacksmith's bellows, and he had a heart as big as Schiehallion itself. I have known him to plunge down a deep gorge after a fallen deer, to scramble up the other side with the beast draped across his shoulders, and his unburdened companions scarcely able to keep pace with him.

On this occasion, Dougal found himself detailed to take out a military commando-training type. They didn't hit it off at the start as men on the hill should, and Dougal found himself being scrutinised from the end of an aristocratic nose, as being pretty poor material.

The pace was a hot one from the start and Dougal was being left behind. His dignity smarted. He, the stalker, should have been piloting the way. With a sharp blast on his staghorn whistle he recalled his athletic guest.

"Look sir," he said, with heavy sarcasm, "we're not supposed to be catching these deer by speed of foot. And, besides, they're seeing you coming a hundred miles away. So we'll just crawl a while." He thought, grimly, a couple of miles on his belly will fix him. But it didn't, and finally Dougal had to call a halt in a small gully.

"We'll bide here for a while," he said, and in silence inspected his bruised pride.

"Wait there a minute," he bade his unruly companion, and scrambled to the top of the rise. Carefully, he parted the tall heather and there, not a hundred yards away, were three stags.

Calmly, Dougal put his spy-glass to his eye and examined them. The nearest was grazing quietly and he dismissed it as an immature beast with a poor head. The other two were clashing antlers in a friendly boxing match.

He was just on the point of making up his mind which of these two it was to be, when the crack of a rifle smote his eardrums, and he saw the young stag he had rejected rise slowly, flail the air with its forefeet and collapse in an inert heap in the heather. The acrid taste of cordite was in Dougal's mouth and a great rage filled his heart.

"What did you do that for?" he bellowed. But the guest paid no heed and mercifully he never head the curses that followed him as he sprinted to do a war whoop around his victim. Dougal walked slowly forward; knife in hand and any onlooker would have been uncertain whether he meant to gralloch the stag or the man. But the stag it was, and as the 'guest' peered exultantly down, Dougal reached up and drew a bloody mark across his forehead.

"What did you do that for?"

"Well sir, it's your first stag."

"That's right. How did you know?"

How did I know! Dougal snarled to himself, and spat disgustedly.

Off they set and the endurance test started all over again, and continued until noon when they met, as arranged, another stalking party to exchange information about the movement of stags, and to have lunch. Dougal envied the other stalker his charge, an elderly, experienced, peaceable man, who would make it a nice day, with the possibility of a five pound note at the end of it. He was stuck with this gigantic greyhound, who would eventually run both their insides out, and leave him nothing but humiliation.

As was customary, the stalkers sat apart from their charges, and Dougal, choking over his bread and cheese, poured out his tale of woe. The other commiserated with him and asked,

"Where will you go this afternoon?"

Dougal made a wild gesture and threw his hands in the air, but stopped there, his eyes fixed on the towering Ben before him. Slowly his eyes travelled down then back up again, up to that formidable top. A grim smile lit up his face. He reached for another sandwich and chewing thoughtfully, said,

"I'm going up there."

"Up where?"

It was the turn of the other stalker to choke. Dougal silently pointed a finger to that distant peak which reached to the fleecy clouds.

"Man, you'll never find deer up there."

"I know that fine, and that's why I'm going."

The other keeper quickly revised his own plans. He wasn't going to miss this bit of fun and he had strong spy-glasses that would give him a good view. He now knew what was on and he chuckled.

He could well remember the sensation Dougal has caused, at the local Highland games, four years before, when he had first stepped forward on his spindly shanks as an entrant for the steep, hill race. All the muscular, athletic boys had taken his presence among them for a joke, but after the starter's gun the laugh was on them.

Their legs and lungs and the red mists swam before their eyes as Dougal mercilessly killed them off, one by one, with his terrific heartbreaking pace. He had bounded down the other side of the hill with the great leaps of a hunted stag, to finish alone. Since then, he had collected the prize money every year and remained undisputed champion.

His unruly charge strode across to the stalkers.

"Well, where do we go now, my man?"

Almost casually, Dougal answered,

"My friend tells me there's a big Royal around the top of the Ben."

"Is there, by Jove! Then let's go."

And he was off, but before he had gone fifty yards, something passed him like a moutain hair. It was Dougal, with all the stops out. From the side of his mouth, he shouted,

"I'll let you know when I see it, sirr."

But his charge was having none of it and was off after him pell-mell. One behind the other, they went up the side of the mountain as though it didn't exist.

Down below, the other stalker gasped and passed his spy-glasses.

"Take a look at that, sir."

"My god!" said the elderly gentleman reverently. "They'll kill themselves. Are they doing it for a bet?"

But Dougal was racing for prestige and revenge. He wasn't out to play with the opposition, he was out to annihilate it.

Two hundred yards from the summit. The pace was now a sizzling, red-hot, gruelling slog. A hundred yards, and Dougal wickedly played his trump card, leading his pursuer on to a stretch of treacherous scree. He skipped like a mountain goat up the sheet of slippery rock fragments, but the sliding stones took the feet from the heavier man.

He stumbled and fell. Frantically trying to get a grip, he rose, scrambling wildly, only to fall again. Up and down, up and down, he struggled on gamely. Dougal looked down from the summit, his chest heaving. He was the falcon, coldly eyeing his prey before descending like a pitiless thunderbolt. He allowed his victim to totter towards him and then admonished.

"You'll have to hurry, sirr, if we're to get that stag before the darkening."

He bounded off, in great curving leaps, down the other side. The poor guest threw himself after Dougal with a stranged sob, but only succeeded in bumping and rolling most of the way, to end up in an exhausted heap at Dougal's feet.

A telephone call from a nearby farmhouse brought Dougal's wife in their little van, with a flask of especially

'laced' coffee for the stricken guest. That got him to his feet and he wove unsteadily round the van to get to the seat in front, but Dougal firmly propelled him to the back.

"My wife will be sitting in front, sirr," and popped him in the back, just as he usually loaded the stags.

Later that night Dougal had a phone call from the laird.

"What have you done with my guest, Dougal? He hasn't come down for dinner."

"Ah, well, sir. I'm thinking he won't be down for dinner tonight. He found the hill a bit hard, but he'll learn, sir. He'll learn."

Dougal went back to his easy chair and slipped off his heavy boots, stretched his feet to the fire, an twiddled his toes luxuriously.

The light faded from the sky, and signalled the finish of the hare shoot. We made our way down from the heights, down to the big farmhouse where steaming bowls of delicious soup and heaped-up plates of meat and potatoes awaited us. How good it was to lean back, free from the talons of the elements, full of good food, warm inside and out.

Dreamily, I listened to the stories of the stags from the men who really knew. This is when the older men come into their own, with the experience that comes with the years.

One seasoned stalker told of the big stag's fight to keep his hinds, of how he continuously circles them, furiously beating off all intruders. In no time at all this magnificent animal will wear himself to a shadow of his former shelf. And how many calves does he sire? Not many. For when he is busy fighting a battle with a challenging stag from the east, another young stag comes in from the west and, to his delight, is met, not with the rearing flail of antler and hooves, but to the delicate ogling of a delicious female!

"That's Nature," said the old man, "just keeping things right." He told us too, about the white stag of Schiehallion. Some have seen it. All have heard of it. But this man knew where it was calved, actually saw the hind leave her newly-born fawn in a circle of old bushy heather. It was a prince among deer, an albino, white as the driven snow.

At first only three knew the secret; the hind herself, the man and a buzzard. The hind never went very far and jealously guarded her treasure, driving off the stealthy approach of the wild cat with blazing eyes and sharp-edged, flint hooves. In the days that followed the youngster grew and flourished, carefully nurtured by the ever watchful mother, moving with her to where the bracken, moss and heather rolled up to a blue summer sky, and down to the valleys when the snow blew around the mountain tops.

Now, wearing his first crown of antlers, the young stag learnt of his greatest enemy — man, and how he stalked the hills, seeking the favour of the winds, the cover of heather and rocks to close in for a shot.

The white prince watched for him, sniffed the air for him and loathed the taint of him. And yet, did not the albino already owe his life to the old man? Had he not stalked the young deer successfully, to send a warning bullet singing through his antlers to make him wilder and warier still, and foil the irresponsible element who, unthinkingly, would seek to destroy such beauty.

Today, flitting ghost-like amongst the corries, this handsome stag faces a future which may be the forerunner of yet another Highland legend, crisply stamping the footprint of reality in a smurr of snow.

19

Winter is the time of the ceilidhs — often spontaneous, arising out of the meeting of good friends, good company and a good dram or two. Sometimes, highly organised, elaborate affairs. But whichever the case, no-one could deny that the people of the straths and glens really know how to enjoy themselves.

They will quickly forego the 'song on a platter' for the true voice, vibrant and direct; turn off the knob that provides potted entertainment from the air, when chance or design offers a ceilidh and earthy contact with folk of their own kind, to laugh and dance and sing among.

For myself, I have a weakness for the story-teller and a story well told. I have in mind the big man from the Islands, who would cradle, in his arms, the newest of babies; arms with the power to crush wrestling opponents to limp puppets, drawn relentlessly to the hairy chest; or send the heavy hammer flying through the air with the ease that one would flick away a spent match; or toss the giant caber with a roar that shook the entire games arena.

Wherever he was, there was a ceilidh. How he chuckled over his Island's tales. The old lady, who frowned deeply upon her cockerel's activities in the hen-run on the Sabbath, and regularly put the bird in solitary confinement on the seventh day. And the day it escaped and was discovered in an amorous embrace with a Buff Orpington hen, the old dame whipped the wretched bird with a tiny ash plant, round and round the run.

"Oho, and she had a fine turn of speed and the cockerel was soon back in jail, minus half his tail." The big frame shook with laughter.

Then he would tell of the thrifty islanders, who made use of everything from the seaweed on the shore that was carried to the fields for manure, to the wrappings on the provisions that the boat brought.

Cloth material was a scarce commodity on the Island at times and there was a tremendous run on a certain brand of flour which came in fine, linen bags. These, the ladies said, made very good pillow-slips, until one night at the New Year's Dance, one of the men birled his partner too enthusiastically and, at the height of momentum, she slipped from his grasp and slid the length of the floor. Gliding on her tummy, her dress billowing over her head, she looked for all the world like a yacht in full sail. And there, sweeping round the curves of her ample bottom were the words TARANTO BEST FLOUR.

But when the mood came over the big man, especially after the drams, which he could tipple as swiftly as a bird swallows a drop of water, the 'Mountain Dew' would set the weaving of this tale:

"It was one night after a late dance. I had just taken home to her croft, the loveliest lassie you ever did see and found, in doing so, I had put twenty miles between myself and home. But that was nothing, many's the time I had walked double, and, it was a fine night.

"I was well into my stride when I found I wasn't alone. Falling into step beside me was a white figure, and that's the truth of it."

Here the story teller paused, his keen eyes under their snowy mantle scanned the audience, to pick out and annihilate any unbeliever. But we were caught up in the spell and found ourselves on that long, lonely walk.

"I wasn't afraid and spoke a soft greeting in the Gaelic, but there was no reply. I tried again in the English which I am not very good at because, you see, I'm thinking in the Gaelic and it makes a cruel mix up of things. But not a word could I get out of it and the silence closed like a stranglehold.

"I bent lower and lower as I walked, until my hand was brushing the surface of the road, on and on, until my fingers closed over the big stone I had been seeking. With all the strength that was in me I hurled the stone at my companion.

"When the mists of effort had cleared from my eyes the white shape was still there and matching me, stride for stride. And in its middle was a big jagged hole where the stone had gone right through!

"Before us the path to home swung to the left and I with it. The white shape, with the jagged hole in the middle, kept to the road and I watched it stride on as the fork of the path and the road wedged us apart. It wasn't until I reached the door of the house that fear was on me and I shook in every limb. The hair on my head stuck out like hedgehog's spines and fairly lifted my bonnet in the air.

"Inside, my father was just making to bed, lighted candle in his hand. I never spoke, but he held the candle up to shed its light on my face. Without a word, he went to the cupboard and poured me a dram.

" 'Now, drink that up. You have seen something tonight?' The fiery liquid settled my chattering teeth and loosened my tongue.

"Yes, it came home with me."

" 'Not home! Where did you leave it, boy?'

"At the fork. It kept to the road at the fork."

" 'Ah, that is good. It had nothing to do with you or me. You didn't touch it, did you?' There was a sharpness in his voice.

"I threw a big stone and it went right through and left a big hole."

" 'The saints preserve us, that was bad. You shouldn't have meddled with it. It would be something for the clachan by the sea. You must never go near it again.'

"I assured him I hadn't the slightest desire to and went to bed.

"But time went by and one day, with my friend Rory, I found myself at the empty clachan. We strode down to the rocky shore and tossed pebbles into the waves and watched the sun set and tint the water a bold red.

"We turned for home, but curiosity stopped us at one of

the cottages. We tried the door, it opened and, groaning at the effort, grudgingly let us in.

"All at once, from the sea, came an angry roaring. It drummed at our ears and ground our bones to dust! We hastily slammed the door and leant against it. The roaring was a gigantic voice, shouting fearsomely in the Gaelic. Then crash! The whole building shook. We lay on the floor, like two lumps of frog spawn. Crash! Crash! Crash! Then silence. A long, long silence.

"When a little of our strength returned we opened the door, only to find the doorway completely blocked with huge boulders, each of them that no six men could lift, the fresh seaweed dripping all over them and the sea fully a hundred yards away.

"Like trapped rats we looked at each other, then, wildly and wordlessly, we flitted out of the little window like frightened bats and flew home."

The big man drew a deep breath and the timbers of the table shuddered as he thumped out his last sentence with a solid hairy fist.

"And every word is true. I'm telling you." And I, for one, believed him.

I was sometimes asked to take the chair at a ceilidh or concert. Although I have always enjoyed myself immensely, and hoped that everyone else did, too, I always felt I was not emotionally constructed for these occasions. This was brought home to me when the local school teacher decided that the time had come to retire. A committee was formed to organise a presentation and farewell party.

Now, this lady had been teaching the children of the strath and glen for over a quarter of a century. She had schooled the children and, in turn, their children, and taken a dedicated pride in her work and I felt, that, besides the material gift, we should try to give something that she would always remember.

So, with the help of a few mothers, and in great secrecy, we gathered the children together, and rehearsed them in the verse of a song.

"Now," I said, "I want you to put everything into this, and if the teacher doesn't bring out her handkerchief, don't any of you look me in the face again."

The children really took this to heart, and the day of the presentation dawned. It was glorious and one that seemed to have been specially reserved for the occasion. One of the lairds made available the grounds of his house, and just to stand there, high on the hill at the top of the glen and look around, was a treat in itself.

There were races, games and ice cream for the children and the ladies of the glen worked their hearts out to provide a sumptuous tea, which was served on the lawns. When the cups had been emptied there came the presentation.

The children grouped together on the terraced grass slopes. Surrounded by a frame of glorious rhododendron blooms they made as pretty a picture as you could wish to see. The speeches were made, the tributes delivered, and on the last word my handkerchief fluttered, like a pigeon leaving a dovecote. It was the signal.

I can hear the voices now, so young and clear, so sweetly sincere:

"Haste ye back, we lo' ye dearly,
  Call again, ye're welcome here,
  May your days be free from sorrow,
  And your friends be ever near.
  And may the path o'er which you wander,
  Be to you a joy each day,
  Haste ye back . . ."

I was crying my eyes out, long before the teacher!

20

Winter was always a challenge. At first it seemed hard to realise that this solid sheet of ice was the self-same serenely blue loch that we had basked beside all summer. Release from the icy grip would only come with the thaw, then we would hear the ice grumble and growl all through the night as its power weakened and the tormented shrieks and groans as the soft wind finally broke its back.

It was also difficult to believe that the banks and braes, now bedded under a heavy blanket of snow had, in the hot, summer sun, reared a myriad of wild flowers.

The cattle ploughed deep, white furrows to their feeding place and, here, the flocks of wild birds came, too, for their 'pickings'. I would recognise those which had sung so sweetly for us in the spring and summer and bid them welcome. There were hungry strangers, too, from far away lands and one morning I called Irralee out to see a flock of snow buntings which had paid us a visit.

We went on to look at the cattle and found one of the heifers in a very agitated frame of mind. The cause was a thick, spiky blackthorn branch which had got deeply entangled in her hairy tail. I distracted the heifer's attention whilst Irralee crept up behind and made a grab at the offending branch.

In a whirlwind of snow the heifer made off, taking Irralee with her. Crouched down, feet together, she slid magnificently, but eventually lost her balance and was towed, sledge fashion, for the next hundred yards! The heifer made a sharp, twisting turn and they parted company. Irralee appeared, white from head to foot. Her gasping words cut through the frosty air and formed misty clouds around me.

"I thought I came to see the snow buntings, not join them!"

"Oh", I said coolly, "I thought you were ski-ing. Do you

know that people pay good money for a tow like that?"

If Irralee hadn't had that blackthorn stick in her hand, I wouldn't have run away!

It was at this time that the rabbit plague, myxamotosis, came to Strathtummel. Nature can be ruthless and cruel in her fashion for her own purposes but, the way I see things, it takes Man to sit down and think up something really hellish.

This struck me most forcibly one night in the woods by the lochside. A February moon was peering coldly through the treetops. Everything was so still that I could hear the faint crackle of the fallen twigs and leaves as the night frost drew them even closer with an icy hand.

All at once there came a curious, shuffling sound, and from the burrows and the treeroots and the cairns of stones crept the victims of the scourge. Rabbits, bodies worn to skeletons, heads swollen twice normal size. A horribly, distorted, stricken race, they crawled aimlessly, sightlessly colliding with trees and stones, blinded and emaciated, waiting only for the final release.

Who, I thought, could witness such a scene and not see in it a terrible warning for mankind. Especially for all who dabble in the diabolical and those who condone it. Tomorrow, the wheeling buzzards would write their message of death in the sky and swoop to clean up the corpses, but not the stain.

Not every one is lucky enough to witness the Dance of the Highland Cattle. I first noticed something unusual when I saw them congregating in the smallest field of the croft, from which the snow was almost clear.

There was something about the cattle's alertness that made me stop and watch as they gradually formed a large circle round the edge of the field. The oldest cow, Dossan Bhuidhe, took up her stance on a little knoll overlooking the rest of the field.

After an expectant hush the dance was led off by Eurach Dearg stepping out round the field, gradually working up to a display of twisting, turning, bucking and rearing, her hooves making muffled drum beats, easing again to a trot round the field to stand quietly in the corner. Whereupon, the next cow set sail, taking in exactly the same circumference, but using her own variety of steps and kicks, finishing with a breathtaking stop beside Eurach Dearg.

The others, in order of 'standing' followed likewise, each animal having its own leaps and bounds to display, right down to the youngest calf, whose thick, woolly coat flopped up and down to the rhythm of her flying leaps.

The whole exhibition was critically surveyed by Dossan Bhuidhe, who has seen fifteen years or more, and who, one would have thought, considered herself past such exuberance. But no, majestically she stepped off her knoll, moving around the circle at an effortless trot and, with gradually increasing speed, until her long, golden hair streamed in the wind.

Then the fireworks really started, with full four-footed bucks, which seemed to gather the ground beneath her and toss it away; she twisted and turned, cleaving the air with her forefeet, her lithe body propelled by muscles of steel, showing off to the 'younger fry' that she was still supreme. She took a full trot round again and stood in the middle to receive a mute, but unmistakeable, acknowledgement that hers was the finest performance of all.

She lowered her great head, with the tremendous span of horn glinting in the blinky sunshine and started to graze quietly, signifying the end of the performance.

The Highland Cattle Dance is said to be the sign of a coming storm and already the dark, snow clouds were piling up behind the mountain ranges to the east, causing a lot of head-shaking and chin-stroking as the 'teuchit storm' is predicted by the folk of the glen.

Driven before it came the curlew with its long, curved beak and plaintive, haunting cry 'curlee, curlee, curlee' echoing and re-echoing among the hills, as it made its way to the moors where the heather is long and the bogs splashed with the green and orange of the spaghnum moss; the black and white oyster-catchers, with their brilliant orange legs and beaks, came sweeping up the loch in tight formation uttering

149

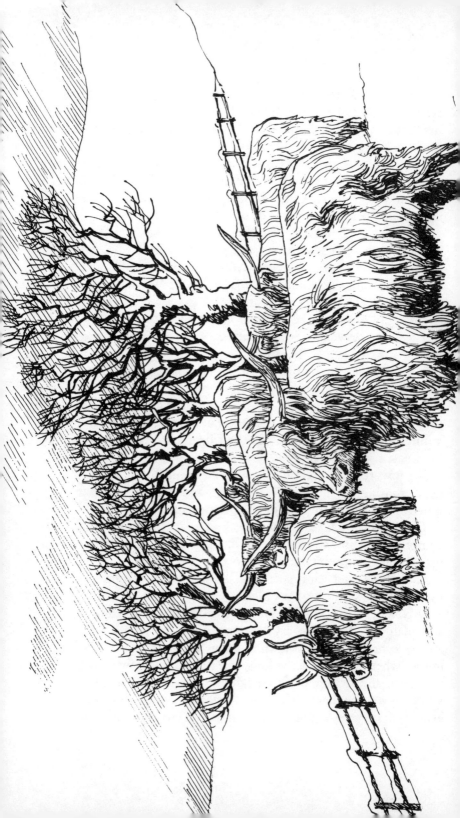

their piping call 'be quick, be quick' as, skimming over the water they came to rest among the multicoloured stones on the shore.

Taking time to exhilarate in its acrobatic abilities, the lapwing with its long, pointed crest and clean cut markings, came winging up to the high land, climbing into the sky letting out that unmistakeable 'pee-weep, weet-a-weet' and tumbled headlong to the earth, its flight feathers spread out like fingers, to turn and skim the ground before flying up again, revelling in the power of its wings, but keeping always a watchful eye on the weather.

Suddenly the mood of the loch changed and it became a dark, menacing grey. The hills on the other side, Meall Tarruin chon, Sròn Mhòr and Creagan Loch disappeared from view behind a curtain of rain and sleet which soon turned to sleet and snow. The curlew up on the moor will have sought shelter in the long-stemmed heather or peat bog, the oyster-catchers will have crept among the big boulders on the shore, and the lapwing or 'teuchit' will have found bield behind some tussock of grass.

The Highland cattle, born and bred to withstand the rigours of our climate with their long forelocks or *dossan* to keep the snow out of their eyes and long hair to drain off the rain and keep their bodies warm, will have sought the shelter of a tree-lined bank. And, in this haven, they remained until the storm was over.

21

Good Fortune must have been looking the other way when its opposite number led my foot astray on a steep rock face and my short cut home turned into a lengthy affair involving a broken ankle and a badly torn ligament. The latter brought home to me that it wasn't my bones that held me together, but the 'strings'.

My leg was slow to mend and gave me a lot of pain. Whenever I was feeling sorry for myself I would look up at the face of Creag Mhor and wonder if I would ever climb it again.

I wondered, too, how I was going to get my young heifers to the market. They were a bonny bunch of lassies and I would love to have kept each and every one, but winter was coming and there were mouths to feed on all sides. I decided to try and find a private buyer and let it be known that my heifers were for sale. I was duly visited by two prospective purchasers.

The first one, after a lengthy discussion on weather, crops and current events, eventually got down to asking about the price. I said I thought thirty pounds each, for them all, was a fair and reasonable figure for my 'blue-blooded babies'. The figure apparently appealed to the buyer who promply selected the best one. I said I was sorry but that was the individual price for anyone taking the lot and I wished to sell them all together.

The second potential buyer treated me to an even lengthier discourse on the state of the world in general and the health of all and sundry, then inquired what I wanted for the heifers. On being told, he pursed his lips, threw a non-committal glance over the young Highlanders and said, in tone of great finality,

"I'll give you twenty-eight pounds apiece."

I know that a lot of folk in the farming line have an asking price and a selling price, but I was not constructed along these lines and had no stomach for bargaining bouts. Besides, I was quite sure my little heifers were well worth the price I had quoted, so I slowly and definitely shook my head.

This buyer, with a wealth of shrewd dealing experience behind him, held his ground with an equal determination. I took a big breath and said,

"All right. I'll take these beasties to Oban and show you that they will make the money."

"Right. I'll follow you there, and maybe I'll get them cheaper."

Gosh, I thought, with my luck the way it is, maybe you will!

When I reported back to Irralee I got a big row for not completing the deal, there and then.

"How", she said, "are you going to get them to Oban? You're far too crippled to walk around the house, let alone drive beasts through the market and the sale ring."

I knew she was talking good sense, but there was a challenge involved and I knew I was going to that market, even if I had to crawl on my hands and knees!

Carefully, I started to plan.

First, I had to find someone to drive me over and give me a hand at the other end. Irralee couldn't do this as there was the croft to look after and the children to see to and from school. I thought of Ewan at the top of the loch. He had always expressed a wish to attend the Oban Sales and here was his chance. Did he want to go? He did.

Next, to organise help to pen and load the animals into the float at this end. I had only to drop a hint to our good neighbours on the west of Croft Douglas. Nothing was ever any trouble — no bother at all. So I ordered the float and awaited, with mounting excitement, the day of the sale.

Our neighbours were the first to arrive and I called to the heifers, still lying somewhere in their heathery beds. They must have thought it a very early call, but soon we heard them coming, then saw them slipping in and out of the birches, like ghosts in the grey light and we had them penned before they knew what was going on.

Ewan arrived next, greetings were exchanged and the pipe and the cigarette glowed.

A pair of powerful lights swept round the bend of the road and the cattle float hissed to a stop beside us then, with a snort, it waddled backwards to the pen. The heifers were getting excited now and surged back. The timbers of the pen groaned under their combined weight, but we coaxed and cajoled and, finally, persuaded them to bound up the ramp.

The float hiccupped contentedly as it felt its belly full then, like a giant refreshed, it rumbled away to the west and Oban, with Ewan and me in close attendance behind it. The journey seemed interminably long and my leg was throbbing with the exertions of the morning.

The tang of the sea, a wheeling seagull and the Gaelic greeting *Fáilte do'n t-Oban* welcomed us. But I no longer felt the thrill of excitement, just awfully sick. Ewan was quite concerned and suggested I stick my head between my knees. It didn't make me feel any better but, on the other hand, I didn't get any worse.

We reached the market and made for the pens. Our big cattle float did another backward paddle, retched a couple of times and disgorged our charges to join the hustle, bustle and general bedlam.

Suckled calves, enduring the first separation from the mothers they loved, bawled their hearts out. The yearlings chafed at the strange confinement and raised their voices in intermittent protest, and, in the sadness of the chorus was all the yearning for the pastures they knew and the hills of home. The older animals accepted their lot with the fortitude that comes with experience, and an occasional mournful bellow.

We gave the heifers some hay to settle them down and when they started eating we set to work with brush and comb. It felt good to be doing something. We combed their soft forelocks so that they tumbled loosely down to pert, pink noses and brushed the long, silken coats to show the wealth of a summer's sunshine and the glint of starry nights. As a finishing touch we teased out the tassels of their tails, making a bouquet from the hair that had brushed the myrtle and the mountain pansy and tangled with the heather.

Above the bovine chorus came an insistent clanging. We gave the little prima donnas a final brush-up. It was for them that the bell tolled. Then, through the clamour came another noise — a human voice, popped into a canister and tossed into the air. It was the outside loudspeakers relaying, from the ringside, the voice of the auctioneer. As if mesmerised by the sing-song chanting the long line of animals and men moved slowly forward towards the arena. We made our way through the pens, gates opened, gates closed, a pause, then the same, again and again.

Three more divisions to go and we had company as two men joined us. One, immaculate in 'fore-and-aft' and duffle coat, questioned me as to the breeding of the heifers. I could see the other question framed in his face, but the talk of money was beneath him, and he called on his companion to utter the query. It came as we moved into the next division.

"How much do you want for them?"

Almost past caring what happened now, I said,

"I don't know, but if you are interested they will be in the ring in a minute or two."

The lines on his face worked pleasantly. "I'll give you thirty-seven a piece for them."

This really startled me. What should I do? As we moved forward again I muttered,

"We've come a long way to put the heifers into the ring, and there is also someone at the ringside to whom I would like to prove a point."

"Thirty eight pounds."

Ewan dug his elbow in my ribs. "It's a good offer," he whispered. Just then the big doors yawned widely, engulfing the heifers and I stumbled after them and leant against the rostrum for support.

A thousand faces, row upon row, built in tiers to the roof,

gazed down upon us then, ever so slowly, they started to revolve in blurred circles. Above me, the auctioneer was off to his mark to get a starting bid.

"Thirty, twenty-five, twenty. Come now, gentlemen, they'll make more. Eighteen then."

I hung my head in humiliation, I really had boobed this time and I tried to console myself that it hadn't been greed for gold that had made me turn a deaf ear to that bid outside the ring. I had only wanted to make a point and I looked like paying for it dearly. My head sank lower and the sawdust rose to meet me, the tiny particles gradually assuming the proportions of rock chips, and faded into timeless sand.

I heard a voice chanting — but with a difference, felt a current of excitement that sparked a fresh charge into my weary body.

"Forty-eight, forty-nine, fifty."

I straightened up.

"Fifty-one."

For the first time in many months I forgot about my leg, forgot the misery and the pain, forgot about the setback to everything we had planned and worked so hard for. Here were my little heifers giving me, in the sadness of farewell, one of my proudest moments. Tightly gripping my stick, I strode out to join them and put them round the ring for the last time.

Like a tumbling wave they swept the ring in front of me, hair flowing, heads tossing, their feet beating a triumphant tattoo.

All in line now, pivoting like Liberty Horses, to top the market for Croft Douglas!

22

The countryside around Croft Douglas is steeped in history, tradition, fact and fiction. The lordly peak at the head of Loch Tummel, home of the ptarmigan, the mountain hare, the stag and the golden eagle, has seen it all. Just climb the slope facing east on a bright, sunny day and watch your shadow flit from one side to the other. Those who profess to know about such phenomena have ventured the opinion that this is caused by refracted light bouncing back from the polished facets of the peak.

But the highland people just shook their heads; they knew what was going on and who was responsible, so they called the mountain Schiehallion, the hill of the fairies. And the Romans, when they marched up to the Highlands, discovered that their shadows were no different to anyone else's and danced to the fairies of Schiehallion.

It is said that Pontius Pilate was born on its lower slopes in the shadow of the oldest yew tree in the world.

The minister of Foss was a keen historian and told me, on one of his visits which always sent Irralee into panic, that he had discovered an old map which showed a Roman encampment on Croft Douglas.

"But", he said, bringing me into focus with his best biblical eye (the right one) "I am not going to show it to you. You will only dig it up and fashion the stones for gain."

I thought this was more than unfair, even from a man of the cloth, especially when I knew, anyway, where the site was and had a coin to prove its authenticity. Along a secret, secluded path lay the sunken walls in a cloak of deep, velvety green mosses that drank heavily of the morning and evening dews and, refreshed, spread themselves again with a soft, lasting caress over the carefully laid stones; the tightly curled fronds of the ferns, so fastidious in picking their spot, traced the line of the site with precision.

In the thickest, most intimate part of the growth, a willow wren had made her nest, a dainty domed structure, so finely built to make even the Romans wonder. I wondered, too, that the minister would ever think me capable of disturbing this peace. But I left him with the feeling that his secret was still locked securely in his care.

We were not regular church goers. The livestock never seemed to appreciate that there was such a thing as the Sabbath, or a seventh day of rest. They just kept on munching their way through one day to the next irrespective of its title.

But this in no way meant that the niceties of respect were entirely forgone at Croft Douglas and, every meal time, tiny chubby hands were laced together earnestly, to prop up the chins of heads that bowed to express appreciation of the food laid before them. Each member of the family knew, or just needed a glance to remind them of their turn to lead the praise.

The minister registered his surprise at my rare appearances in the House of God by almost tumbling out of his pulpit. He knew I wasn't baptised, because I had told him, and sought his help as I wanted to give my children the opportunity which I had been told would be denied to me, of approaching the kingdom of heaven.

I tried to explain that my parents had their own faith which did not recognise the Holy Ghost and I was instructed in the nicest possible way, that it just did not exist. The minister was unimpressed and left me in no doubt that, if I wished a child baptised, the Ghost would have to be present.

"But," he said, opening a door for a possible way out, "if, as I understand, you wish to remain loyal to the teachings of your parents, your wife can repeat the required incantation," and, so saying, flung his arm aloft to receive acclamation from above for his resolving of the problem. But it didn't come.

The fickleness of woman is a permanent wonder to me and Irralee quickly decided where her loyalties lay, which brought home to me just how valuable were her opinions to me.

That evening I called on the minister to tell him to forget all about it for the meantime. He couldn't have been kinder and, as we bid each other good night, he leaned towards me and said,

"I do admire your principles, because I," and he glanced over his shoulder, "do not believe in the immaculate conception."

I wasn't too sure about that, but received a call from the minister of the next parish. Was it to do with christenings, I wondered? But, no, he asked me to meet him at the Atholl Arms to discuss a proposed ceilidh at Killiecrankie. We were just supping each other's drams in the luxurious comfort of the lounge, when the head-waiter, his shirt front like a swan's, glided towards us.

"A Highland gentleman's compliments and would you join him in the dining-room?"

We followed the immaculate tails along the tartan carpets to the large, impressive dining room. Stags' heads, regally antlered, gazed dispassionately down from the balcony and, displayed around the walls in glittering array, was the armament of the highlander: breast plates, targes, broadswords, claymores, battle axes and dirks.

But, surely in their day, the clash of those weapons never exceeded the clatter of cutlery that now greeted us! Hundreds of knives and forks squeaked and grated as they carved their objectives and skidded across the glaze of the plates, which screamed aloud at the torture.

We were deftly piloted to a centre table and greeted enthusiastically by the H. G. who, with a circle of friends, had wined and dined and wined again. With them, we drank too and there arose a great discussion around the historical events of these parts, and, in particular, the armoured breast-plate of Claverhouse, the Viscount of Dundee, which the party had been viewing that day.

The H. G. launched into his account of the story that lay behind the breast-plate. Step by step we were taken up the Pass of Killiecrankie with the forces of William and Mary, who had been called to the British Throne. There is the Trooper's Well, so called because one of the cavalry officers stopped to water his horse, only to tumble in himself, the recipient of a highlander's bullet. But the army pressed on, a formidable force of infantry, cavalry and cannon.

Pouring out from the head of the Pass they saw, on the hill before them, the army they had come to destroy, the highlanders who sought to fight for the exiled Stuart king and, at their head mounted on a black charger, the gallant Dundee.

For two hours Dundee restrained his restless, kilted warriors. Not that he hesitated to attack an army more than twice as large as his own. Claverhouse, the Viscount Dundee, waited for only one reason — the brilliant afternoon sunshine was in his eyes. Just before sunset he ordered his men to throw aside their plaids and, raising his sword, gave the battle cry.

The lowland army, ranged shoulder to shoulder must have marvelled at this sight before them and felt their blood curdle at the mad skirl of the bagpipes as the highland clans charged down the hill, a wild, colourful wave lit by the setting sun. The cannon roared, the rifles cracked and spat volley after volley, but nothing could stop this tartan torrent as it swept over the infantry, the cannon, the cavalry, and engulfed them in a swirl of flashing broadswords and claymores.

At this point the H. G. paused to down his dram and I suddenly realised how quiet everyone was. The entire population of the dining-room, mostly visitors from the South, were breathlessly following the tale.

The H. G. brought us back to the mopping up stage of the battle and the Balfour Stone. Against this stone, he said, a Brigadier-General Balfour fought for his life, attacked simultaneously by two brawny highlanders. A Highland chieftain came up at that moment and called out in Gaelic, "Shame. Give the brave man his life," and courteously addressed the Brigadier. But Balfour's reply was an unprintable insult and the young chieftain strode forward, angrily, and literally cut the officer in two with a mighty stroke of his claymore.

The H. G. mopped his brow in horrified ecstasy and made the solemn announcement,

"And they say that the deep red score down the face of the stone was made by the blade of the claymore."

There was a silence while this was digested, then the H. G. was off again, painting a vivid picture of the victorious highlanders as they pursued the fleeing army and the fugitive made his escape, and history, by desperately leaping the gorge over the River Garry.

"And", continued the H. G. "the 'Soldier's Leap' it has been called ever since. If you don't believe such a jump is possible just imagine you have a pack of highlanders with bloody broadswords, on your tail!"

Then the H. G. took us back to the garden of Urrard House, where Dundee was letting his horse drink from a spring when, from a window of the house, a shot rang out and a sleek, silver bullet penetrated a joint in his armour, Claverhouse, Viscount of Dundee, slowly fell from the saddle to the soft green Urrard turf and with him, the Cause of King James of Scotland.

Here the H. G. almost sobbed as he quoted,

"Here sank the warrior stricken
By charméd silver ball,
And all the might of victory
Dropped nerveless in his fall".

The H. G. was silent for a moment and the entire diningroom grieved with him. Then he raised his head and ran his eyes around our table.

"You have all seen Claverhouse's breast plate?"

We all nodded.

"Then what manner of man do you think it would fit?"

Various suggestions were made but the H. G. swept them contemptuously aside.

"There is only one man *here* could wear that breast plate".

I wondered who it could be. We were a mixed company,

tall, short, fat, broad, lean. I gasped in horror as the H. G. pointed an unwavering finger straight at me. Hundreds of eyes 'coned' me in a merciless spotlight.

"And do you know why?"

The H.G's voice had reached full pitch and he paused long enough to allow everyone a good mouthful of unadulterated silence. The multitude leaned in towards our table, as flowers seeking the light. At last it came.

"Because his chest goes down to his navel!"

The minister, with a deep chuckle, patted me on the back three times that silently spelled out his inability to decide whether to commiserate or congratulate, then with a ticklish whisper in my ear,

"I will pick you up for the ceilidh tomorrow at seven".

He arrived in a car that wheezed gently to a stop but kept its engine going with a religious chug, chug, chug, allowing me time only to scramble in before we took off down the Tummel road.

Sitting serenely in the centre of a field on our right, is a small graveyard with only three headstones; a place of quiet substance, sheltered and surrounded by a stout five foot wall, without a crack or hole in its structure and no hiding place for a beetle, let alone a weasel. This wall was built with a purpose that would take no notice of the passing of time. Its only entrance is by a heavy iron gate. The headstones speak silently of the mortal remains that lie beneath them.

There are Frasers and Stewarts, who have lain here at Borenich since eighteen hundred and thirty one, their ages ranging from a tender three years to a ripe seventy-two. There is a small iron cross with a celtic design and, fashioned in large letters across the centre bar, the word 'Kirsty'. Flanked by the headstones Kirsty sleeps serenely in the middle. She has no surname and remains ageless, for her time has long ago ceased to matter. Was she a lady, or a hand-maiden, or just a little serving girl who was highly thought of? Someone thinks of her to this day, for the hallowed spot is carefully tended.

We muse together, the minister and I, 'here today but where tomorrow?' But at this moment, we are still in the minister's faithful car, the one that carried an ecclesiastical insurance that all the other cars would give their cylinder heads to own; the sparking plugs have a hymn of their own and, as we passed along the lonely road, our thoughts turned to the waters of Loch nan Nighean (Loch of the Maidens) high above us, secluded in the hills.

This is a spot that a maiden dare not approach but, if there is one with the boldness to seek adventure, one who dares to put her dainty foot near the water's edge, the legendary white stallion is sure to surface in a wild wash of foam and lie down at the edge of the water. His magnetism will draw the maiden to climb upon his back and the stallion, claiming her for his own, sinks contentedly to the depths of the loch with his precious burden, who will never be seen again.

I confided to the minister that, in relating the legend to a certain lady, she had slowly shaken her head and said, with a depth of feeling,

"I don't think I'll have anything to fear from that beastie!"

My dog-collared companion seemed to slip his leash and revel in an appreciation of the moment when freedom of expression comes like the bubbling call of the curlew. It is said, here, that the curlew carries the soul of a being who has been refused admission to heaven or hell, and has found everlasting life in the heather of the highlands.

The minister's big hearted machine was carrying us towards the river gorge and the spot where Robert the Bruce spent the night. He wasn't watching spiders on this occasion. He and his men were resting, exhausted, after the Battle of Methven Moor. Here, the crofters demonstrated what highland hospitality is all about. They fed the king and his warriors hot broth and bowls of porridge. Ever after, the place was known as Coille brochain (Wood of the porridge).

But it was to be a while before I sampled the morning porridge. We had now reached the Killiecrankie village hall, scene of all social activities in the district. The minister's car made a great huffing and puffing to find a parking place. I was hesitant about giving advice to a pillar of the church but, in a brave effort to resolve the situation said,

"There's a space over there".

My suggestion, like the unprofitable seed, fell, not only on stony ground, it stotted around unwelcome and unwanted. After a deal of coming and going and grating of gears, I was secretly pleased to hear the sanctimonious conveyance squeal under the lash of the minister. Finally, the car was parked to his satisfaction, then and only then, he said,

"This, Gideon, is the first lesson when attending a ceilidh. Always point your nose to home".

The custodians of the hall had very strict rules about the type and strength of liquid to be consumed in the building; parsley, blackcurrant, apple and dandelion wines were darkly frowned on and spirits were definitely banned. This posed all sorts of problems for the artistes appearing, who felt in need of a little support if they were to give of their best. Painstakingly Alisdair, the piper, and Colin, the accordionist, both of them blessed with all the physical endowments a bounteous Nature could bestow, were covered with a shyness that was painful to witness.

But sharing this distressing complaint had led to an understanding. They had come prepared; Alisdair with a half bottle of malt whisky and a screwtop in his pipecase and Colin, in his accordion box, had a bottle of 'the Best'.

The minister and I were sharing the position of 'Fear an tighe' (man of the house) in charge of all proceedings, and the hall was packed to suffocation. I took a deep breath, stood up to give the audience a traditional welcome, then called upon Alisdair to give a blow of the pipes to start the evening.

Alisdair was resplendent in the Atholl tartan and his plaid swung gaily as he made turns in the march to and fro on the platform. This reminded me of a Pipe Band parade in Pitlochry. Alisdair had been peat cutting all that day. It was a deep, clammy bog, he was working in so he wore his heavy corded trousers and, for good measure to keep out the wet and cold, underneath a pair of long, woolly, white drawers.

He had left it very late, stacking the peats to dry, and had to hurry to reach the parade on time. Quickly, he cast off his jacket and cords and, to save time, rolled the long drawers well up above his hairy knees, strapped on his kilt, wound on his plaid, slipped on a pair of brogues, grabbed his pipes, and raced to the meeting place at Pitlochry railway station, just in time to take his place in the front line before the Drum-Major sang out the order to march.

It was the height of the tourist season and the pipe band parade was to be a special evening treat for the visitors, and it really was! As the band swept round into Pitlochry Main Street, filling the air with the roll of the drums and the blood-stirring music of the pipes, each smack of Alisdair's brogues on the roadway brought the long drawers creeping down, until they reached his ankles. The crowd gazed in amazement as they witnessed the answer to that age-old question. Alisdair, being a sensible man, ignored the gales of laughter that erupted from the crowds and endured the leg-pulling of his fellow pipers. But that was a long time ago.

Alisdair finished his piping selection with a stormy rendering of 'Scotland the Brave', and smartly saluted in acknowledgement of the waves of applause. But he was not finished yet. He had to stand by for the highland dancing. Pipers who play for highland dancing are few and far between, a breed all of their own with the ability to link their music with the twinkling toes of the dancer. And, tonight we had two dancers.

The first was waiting, her dainty feet one moment matching the poise of the humming bird and the soft, fleeting kiss of the butterfly and the next, the determination and vigorous shake of the leg this particular dance demanded. This dance was the Seann Truibheas, which evolved after the '45 Rising, when the Jacobite cause fell, blood-stained and exhausted. The victor, unlike the Romans, showed no mercy after a good fight and banned the sound of the bagpipes, the language and, worst of all, the wearing of the kilt. The dance was the highlanders' haughty reply.

They hated the trousers and longed to cast off all the restraining influences and shackles that had been imposed by an unrelenting foe. The dance spelt it all out and the audience was ecstatic.

I felt parched and longed for liquid of any kind. I glanced at the minister's glass of ginger ale, flanked by two bottles of Schnapps. The minister excused himself to find the whereabouts of Colin, the accordionist and, with a glance around, I regaled myself with a sip from the minister's glass. It had a kick that would make any self-respecting mule sulk in envy. I knew, in this moment, that the minister had found his own way of beating the rules and regulations — but who was I to question it. The result, as far as I was concerned, was very pleasant, and helped considerably in the rendering of my favourite yodelling song.

The minister was still absent in his search for Colin and I called upon the next artiste, Mairi. She was a formidable female and full of Gaelic, of her own teaching and not learned at her mother's knee, and she knew what ceilidhs were all about. She held the accolade of a Mod Gold Medal and, in our now liberated society, had often held the office of Bean-an-tighe (Lady of the House). Tonight she was in frivolous vein, and, before her song, told a story I hadn't heard before. It was about two old farmers returning from the market, who had the misfortune to run over a white hare. This, to anyone in their sober senses would be a tragedy and an omen of bad luck, but to the inebriated farmers, it was a disaster.

They tried to revive the stricken animal with body massage and the kiss of life, but to no avail. Then one of the farmers produced a bottle from his jacket pocket and poured a generous sample down the hare's throat. At once the animal sat up, shook itself so hard that its ears flapped together and bounded joyfully away up the mountain side. The other farmer asked,

"What was in the bottle?"

I could not restrain myself.

"It was hair restorer," I blurted out.

Everyone cheered except Mairi. She turned on me with the savagery of a she cat defending her young.

"You," she said, "you have spoilt my story."

The crowd loved it and shrieked for more and Mairi, with a single glance, left me in no doubt that I, and all my ancestors, as far as she was concerned, could rot in hell. Then taking a deep breath which saw her chin disappear into the divide that separated her generous bosoms, she gave vent to her feeling in a soul seeking version of Morag of Dunvegan. The audience joined in the choruses, which saw the roof of the Killiecrankie hall strained to its limits. Amidst the storm of applause and, in her triumph, Mairi turned and gave me a kiss — I was forgiven!

The minister sat down beside me, took a deep sip from his glass, apparently unaware that it was somewhat lowered.

"There's no sign of Colin. Go and see what you can do."

I found him in a remote ante room, stacked with desks and chairs. He was a desperately shy man, was Colin, and should never have been exposed to the ordeal of performing before people. But I reminded him that he was committed; the posters in the hotels, on the public notice boards and on the tree trunks said he would be appearing.

"Yes, yes," he said. "But I have not yet had enough," and the neck of the bottle disappeared as his lips embraced it. I left him to the final preparation for his ordeal.

I had a quick look across the stage to see how the minister was coping. He was introducing the next highland dancer. She was one I knew well, in a class of her own, with long, dark hair and high celtic cheek bones. She could swear so delicately that you didn't even notice, and she used words that I hadn't heard of. Her speciality was the Sword Dance, a dance very close to the highlander's heart. After the cut and thrust and blood-letting of battle, when he found himself alive and victorious, he drew his sword and, laying it on the ground across its sheath danced in triumph over the naked blade.

Morag's toes danced in and out of the shining sharp steel with a wild abandon that had everyone sitting on the edge of their seats.

Dougie was next. He was the magician and the audience held its breath in anticipation. He always, on occasions like this, had a brand new trick. What would it be? Meantime, Dougie was going through his opening routine of pulling out an endless line of flags of all nations from his pocket finishing with the Lion Rampant.

He was working up to the big one and was spinning a coin from hand to hand.

"Where is it now?" he asked, showing two empty hands.

"Where . . ." he started again. He choked and his face turned purple. I knew something had gone wrong and smote him heartily between the shoulder blades.

Out flew the coin and tinkled noisily among the footlights. The crowd thought it was all part of the act and were delighted. Dougie was now working up to his grand finale. I glanced down at two circular tins. The lid of one suddenly became agitated and opened to reveal first the nose, then the head of a tiny black and white rabbit.

"Dougie," I whispered anxiously, but he did not hear me. I tugged his long coat and nearly released a white dove which was roosting in the inner pocket. Dougie condescended to turn his head round and glare at me over his shoulder.

"The rabbit," I said, "It's going to escape."

Dougie was blessed with a fantastic pair of lips and a mouth that could speak to the audience with one side and to me with the other. The message I got was

"Give the little blighter a carrot."

I searched around and sure enough, found a carrot. I popped it quickly in beside the jail breaker, the lid subsided and clicked into place, and now Dougie was saying,

"I am going to bake a cake."

Calm as you please he turned to me and said,

169

"Could you oblige me?"

I held up the two tins.

"Now", he said, lifting the lid of the first one then the other, "you have examined these two tins and found them empty". He said it with such conviction that the tiny bunny tucking into the carrot must have been a figment of my imagination.

"Yes", I said, "they are empty".

With a dexterous move Dougie put the bunny tin to the bottom and cracked eggs and flour into the other one. With his magic wand stirring the mixture he raised his eyes to the ceiling. When everyone was looking up at the ceiling he switched the tins again, tapped the lid smartly with his wand, lifted the lid and to thunderous applause, lifted out the little black and white rabbit.

I found that supporting Colin was heavy work and guided him towards a chair in the centre of the stage. He sank upon it as if encamped for the night with a deep, soul-satisfying 'hic'. Then he began to play. Colin read no music and played only by ear, but tonight he was under the spell of the uisge-beatha; he was a man possessed of something that he had to share with others.

His final performance of 'Dear, old mother, mine' had the place awash with tears, and they called for him again and again.

It was then that Colin made his big mistake. He heaved himself from the chair and, not allowing for the weight of his accordion, staggered forward to the edge of the stage and bowed to the audience. He somersaulted and made a fortunate soft landing on the laps of the people in the front row.

On the way home the minister turned to me and said,

"Gideon (he pronounced it Guid yin). Oh, Guid yin, it was a grand ceilidh, was it not?"

23

There was no dearth of real characters in and around the valley.

Jeannie had served in the Women's Royal Army Corps during the war and when her reference said that Jeannie had served it meant, in her case, that the tasks given to her had been well and truly attended to. She had returned to life on the croft seasoned by her experiences and met every day with the supremely optimistic view that she would live forever with this in mind.

She milked the goats, fed the hens, wrestled with the crops and looked after her ageing father, long ago made a widower, but noted for his fishing escapades up loch and down river where he sought the peace and tranquillity such places bring. He had more experience than any other fisherman in the valley having once wrestled with the biggest salmon ever to enter the waters of Loch Tummel. It happened that one day he was casting his favourite fly, the colourful Thunder and Lightning, across the waters of the loch, letting it drift gently with an occasional flick of the rod to give the lure a semblance of life, its beauty, provided by feathers of jay, the grouse and the golden pheasant. Suddenly, the reel screamed in agony as the lure sped out with the speed of a lightning strike.

Jeannie's father knew, in that moment, that he was shaking hands with the biggest fish he had ever met. Already the beads of sweat were meeting on his brow. The fish broke water in a flashing arc of blue and silver, amply demonstrating that he was straight from the sea and sporting the lice to prove it. Down, down he went, to rid himself of the lure that had tempted him in a moment of weakness when he had found, on tasting it, it was a trick to rob him of his life.

How this gigantic fish fought! And how his adversary, the old man, thinking this his finest moment fought back, by skilfully playing the monster salmon, giving extra line when he asked for it, then taking it away again to bring the tiring fish closer. Then came the instant that found them both weary of the struggle and, guided by the rod, the salmon slid into a side pool near the bank.

The old man was in a frenzy of excitement. His net had not been made big enough to hold this fish and he had no steel gaff with which to make the deadly strike. What could he do? He looked down and then came the answer. His wooden leg! With rod held high, he slipped off his wooden leg and used it to tenderly steer the fish into shallow water. Then throwing rod and caution to the winds, he plunged upon the salmon. Together they wrestled, locked together in a desperate fight; one to gain the prize of a lifetime, the other for life itself.

Then, finally, the great fish, in one sleek, slithering, muscle-bending movement, back-somersaulted from the old man's determined grasp, spat out the remains of the Thunder and Lightning, and leapt back to the deep water to race on its way, rejoicing, to keep its date with destiny.

The old man stumped homewards, disconsolate, and cried on Jeannie's shoulder about the loss of the king fish, but Jeannie was not impressed and sat him down at the table and dished up a savoury stew prepared from a rabbit she had caught that had been foolish enough to break into her garden and devour the cabbage.

Jeannie was strong. There were few men who would care to tangle with her unless in an amicable embrace. She had a little Ford and had once sent for a reconditioned engine to give it new life. It duly arrived and was left at Strathtummel Post Office. Jeannie called for it, ripped apart the wooden crate and, gathering the engine in her stout, freckled arms, carried it for half a mile, straight up the hill.

On being asked if she was ever married Jeannie would laughingly reply,

"Mony a time, mony a time, but never was I kirkit".

Tormaid, from across the loch, had his eye on Jeannie. He was single and tired of living alone and doing for himself. He had also, when lending a hand with the hay, partaken of

Jeannie's breakfast — a huge bowl of porridge with lashings of creamy milk from her goats, whose greatest delight was to soundly butt Jeannie's generous bottom whenever she bent down. The porridge was followed by a huge plate with two orange yolked fried eggs, two fat sizzling sausages, two thick, mouth-watering rashers newly cut from the ham hanging from the ceiling, blood red steaming tomatoes and tender, succulent field mushrooms on a bed of golden brown fried bread.

With a series of such breakfasts in mind Tormaid warmed to his courtship. But Jeannie was unmoved, particularly when one day Seumas called to enquire if there was anything she needed.

"Yes." she replied, ruefully eyeing the masses of chickweed in her garden, "have you any hoe heads?"

Seumas rushed home and could only find his own hoe, but cheerfully cut off the head and took it to Jeannie, who surveyed the newly sawn-off stump.

"You are a silly booger!"

Jeannie was always good to the tinkers. It is said that when they call at a house, they always leave a secret mark behind, as a sign to the next member of the fraternity who passes that way. It tells what kind of reception and hospitality to expect. Usually it was a handful of pebbles arranged to spell out the message. Here, there was milk and sugar in the tea, hot scones with the butter melting in them and maybe a piece of home-made cheese. In some places the message was no so good, it was a home of hard crusts, mysterious or runny 'jeelly' or, worst of all, a door shut firmly in the face.

But Jeannie was called upon regularly and honoured, on occasions, by the queen of the clan, reputed to have second-sight. She was a dab-hand at reading the tea-leaves and the cards and rejoiced in the unsalubrious name of Sweaty Kate. One dark November day she gazed long and earnestly into Jeannie's cup and announced in a solemn far-way voice,

"There is a loss coming your way".

And, sure enough, the very next day, Jeannie's father

decided to embark on the long sleep. It was customary to call, condole and take a last look at the departed. I was ushered into the back parlour with its stuffed birds, china dogs and 'wag at the wa'' clock. There, in the centre, the old man lay in a halo of serenity wearing the peaceful, cherubic look of a sleeping choir boy.

A tear dropped down onto the oaken edge of the coffin and slowly trickled down its side. I turned and looked at Jeannie, surprised. I had never thought, even in a situation such as this, to see her cry. Fiercely, she brushed one hand across her cheek and with the other grasped the little goatee beard and gently rocked the old man's head to and fro, crooning softly,

"You look smashing, just smashing, you lovely old booger".

Relatives and friends all met at the churchyard and so many drams had already been supped that two friends nearly fell into the open grave reaching across it to shake hands. Everybody was there, grand parents, aunts and uncles, brothers and sisters, cousins and half cousins and some who, by now, were only half sure if they were there at all and, floating discreetly in the background, were Sweaty Kate and two handmaidens.

The minister, book in one hand and glass in the other, gave an elegant tribute and led the hymn singing; the bagpipes dwelt for a moment on a sad lament then broke into a foot-tapping reel that spoke of joyful moments to come, more drams, and bannocks to soak them up, with a ceilidh to follow into the early hours. The old man would have loved his hilarious send-off and the occasion fully justified the old saying,

"A funeral in Strathtummel is worth a wedding in Rannoch".

Little Old Uilleam, was not only the salt of the earth, in his lifetime he had given his all to the soil; his youth, his muscle, the very flesh of his bones and now, with his back bent and a fragile frame he faced up to the last years of his life with a light that twinkled merrily in his eyes. Those long years had left him with a priceless gift, a complete understanding of animals. The proud, uncontrollable stallion that bowed to no-one else ate quietly from his hand. Horses and Uilleam were a blend of their own.

Every Saturday when the toil of the week was at an end, bar the tending of the livestock, he would harness up his favourite mare. They knew each other's every move and frequently held long, intimate conversations in the stable. Sally was the patient, loving, understanding mate that he had always yearned for.

It mattered not how long she had to wait in the yard of the hostelry, she knew that Uilleam was savouring every sip of the glass and every moment of the good company, but would not forget her. She could almost time, to the second, when he would appear with a pint of stout. The foaming bubbles tickled her nostrils before she drank, long and deep. Uilleam gave her a fond pat and said,

"I won't be long".

But Sally had heard all this before and rested her legs alternately for the long wait, while the stout made comforting conversation in her belly. When the moment came that Uilleam decided, at last, it was time to go home and staggered uncertainly towards the trap, hung on the side unable to make the step up, Sally knew exactly what to do. With a friendly nuzzle she gently and smoothly wormed her nose between Uilleam's pliable legs and, with a toss of her head, despatched him safely into the bottom of the cart. With a snort of satisfaction she set off for home with a sharp clip-clop.

Uilleam's big Aberdeen-Angus bull had a deep and lasting hatred for the young upstart that answered his challenge from the nearby fields. They bawled and called until surprisingly and suddenly, they found themselves in adjoining fields, facing each other across the march dyke. The young bull roared what must have been a deeply insulting remark proving too much for the big fellow who, literally, bull-dozed the stone dyke with his massive chest and got to grips with his adversary.

This was the beginning of the father-and-mother of all bull fights; the old one seeking to maintain his authority over the herd and the young one in with a roaring challenge to take over. The earth shook with their clashing heads, the cloven hooves were cruelly directed to tear apart the bellies of the antagonists. Each attack was accompanied by thunderous roars, pig-like squeals and fearful snorts of rage. It was a terrifying battle and made no pretence of being anything else but a battle to the death.

There were people on the scene now, strong men armed with pitch forks, but the bulls were not to be separated. As far as they were concerned this fight could only end one way. The heads crashed in a bone-crushing crunch and the young bull staggered under the knock-out blow and sank to his knees. With a scream of triumph the big bull, completely ignoring a vicious and concerted pitch fork attack, knelt on the fallen one, a series of roars revolving in his throat. His intention was crystal clear — to grind the insides of his opponent to pulp.

Little Uilleam rushed forward to the raised backside of the big bull and, quickly stripping a leather lace from his boot, tied it tightly around the neck of the pendulous bag containing the bull's fertility tokens. with a grunt of surprise and dislike the big bull rose unsteadily to his feet, his fire on the point of extinction. Uilleam clipped a rope into the bull's ring as the animal snorted in defeat.

Uilleam gave the rope a twitch to remind the old bull that he was now 'had' at both ends and added,

"We'll be going home now. And you", he said, with a direct stare into the eyeballs of the bull, "will just be very canny with the old man".

The bull went quietly and, almost on tip-toe, followed him home. Oh, yes, he knew all about animals, did Uilleam.

24

Everybody in the valley respected Garry because of his special gift. The best field of the croft was always given over to the growing of barley which provided the raw material. No-one in or out of Tummelside knew better than he how to perfect a drop of the magical uisge beatha. They said, in hushed whispers, that he had been left the secret recipe by his grandfather, who had always had the feeling that the laddie was part of himself and so, on his deathbed, he asked for Garry.

Not a word passed between them, just the clasp of hands, but in the last farewell there was a message, a folded paper pressed firmly into Garry's hand. It was the message revealing the magic touch required to produce the perfect potion. He was certainly the favoured one to have a last handout of this nature and Garry only needed to tend and look after the field of barley.

His other needs for the croft, hay and turnips for the animals, potatoes and oats for himself, came from neighbours, near and far, and each load was exchanged for a bottle of the best.

There was no colouring in Garry's brew. It was as clear as the burn water; an instant cure for the toothache, for the anxious waiting for a letter or any problem life had to offer; it was a balm to the grieving over the loss of a loved one and the best of company to those, who at times, felt themselves in the cold impersonal grip of loneliness. Garry was never lonely, for men, and, discreetly, some of the ladies, beat a path to his door.

He had had a colourful career and had served in the second world war but there being an independent soul, had found the discipline hard to take. He soon became acquainted with the inside of the guardroom and, in spells of incarceration, thought only of escape. And when he wasn't in the guardroom there was an officer who valued his services as a batman and used his high ranking influence to bail him out.

But even this was of no avail the day he was stopped by two military policemen and questioned closely about his lack of a leave pass and what he was doing out and about. Garry did not have the answers and when clasped on his shoulder with the firm authority of his red-banded arm, Garry quickly came to the boil. With a straight left and a crossed right, he felled his two would-be captors. Garry was now 'on the run'.

Fortunately, he was resourceful, and obtained his sustenance by frequenting the eating houses and bars, quickly clearing up a plate that was, for the moment, being ignored or a drink, that stood neglected whilst its owner was engaged in argument or discussion. Garry knew exactly how the jackdaw and magpie made a living and now, with five pints of assorted lagers and beers and the eldorado of a large whisky, apparently without an owner and, wonder of wonders, a steaming, golden dish of fish and chips whose intended devourer had suddenly found a need for the toilet, he had done well.

He turned his coat collar up as a shield against the chill of the night. But where to sleep, where to lay down his head that now was filled with a heavy weariness? The answer came out of the darkness. Garry walked straight into the arms of a military patrol.

Sharing the guardroom with him were three other A.W.O.L.s. One, a former mechanic to trade, had something special in the way of a miniature screwdriver and, when the cloak of exhaustion hung heavy on the guards and their shoulders drooped in sleep, Garry got busy unscrewing the hinges of the guardroom door. The special screwdriver worked like a charm and Garry stepped outside with a sigh of satisfaction. He was, once again, free.

"Are you coming with me?" he asked the others but they, feeling they were in trouble enough already, slowly and sadly shook their heads.

"Right", said Garry, replacing the door and handing back

the instrument of release, "do me a favour and screw it up again?"

So saying, he was gone into the night but his freedom was to be short lived.

The very next day, in a sleazy back street pub, he was caught in the act of pinching a sailor's pork pie and pint. A furious battle followed in which Garry and the sailor were locked in anything but a friendly embrace, rolling over and over in the beer-sodden sawdust. The twin doors opened and through them burst the military patrol, who had been hastily summoned by the landlord.

Once more he was deposited at the guardroom but, this time, in to a special cell for persistent escapees. His escort pleaded with him to explain how he had escaped but Garry just smiled and murmured,

"Just watch me get out of this one" so giving his guard a sleepless night. He got out all right, but in the morning and in the most unexpected way.

His officer, who was being sent to the front line, had obtained a special dispensation for Garry and his services. The high ranking authorities, in their wisdom, figured that Garry would find enough trouble there to keep him fully occupied. They were right, and Garry fully justified his officer's faith in him.

The officer had failed to return from a night patrol when he had set out in darkness in the hope of snatching a prisoner with some information but, instead, they stumbled on a hornet's nest and found themselves in a hand to hand battle with knives, bayonets and fists.

Garry questioned the returning survivors and was told the officer had ordered his patrol to return to base and was last seen giving them covering fire.

There was still the cover of darkness and Garry vanished into it. He dared not use a light but, like a cat, stalked back and forward with feverish anxiety. Would he find his officer before the new day that was already blinking its waking eyes to betray the slightest movement?

Garry looked up at the top of the tall fir trees taking shape in the morning light and they seemed, silently, with pine laden arms, to be waving him away with agitated gestures, from the danger that they so unwittingly concealed. Garry fell into a fern-choked ditch and tripped over the blood-soaked body of his officer. He bent down, his throat constricted by the cords of emotion. Ripping open the soaking tunic he laid his head on the bloody chest. There was a feeble heartbeat — he was alive! At this moment, the officer opened his eyes and whispered,

"Get to hell out of here. That is an order".

"Aye," Garry said, "and you are coming with me, surr. Who else is going to take the trouble to get me off the hook?" And, so saying, he gently manoeuvered the officer's body across his back. He wasn't a heavy man, Garry had carried heavier stags many a time so, locked together, they began one of the most dangerous journeys of all, across the shell-torn, blood-soaked hell of no-man's land.

Garry was making excellent progress, but time and the light of day were against him. From the wood gutteral cries were ground out and a hail of bullets whined over and around them. Garry never heard the one that smacked into his shoulder. He sank silently to his knees and prayed in the Gaelic to the only One he knew would care, for the strength to go on. And so, with their blood mingling, Garry found the strength he needed and rose, unsteadily, with his burden.

Then happened the miracle. The enemy, lining the woods with enough fire power to wipe out a thousand Garrys, ceased firing and gave, with those silent guns, a salute to such courage as this. Step by step, with his heart beats ringing in his ears, the red mist blinding his eyes and the salty taste of blood in his mouth, Garry kept going until willing hands pulled them both to safety and life.

Garry had fought his way to an honourable discharge and then returned to life on the croft. It was lying there waiting for him, everything just the same, with the bog myrtle making shy promises to the heather, and the curlew wheeling overhead. But, sadly, for the community, the Excise men were listening to whisperings in the wind and were well and truly on the trail.

Garry's grandfather had served his time as a stone mason and, in the house he claimed from his father, had created his masterpiece, the hearthstone. Three hundredweight of green veined marble from the River Tilt lay polished and snug in front of the fire. Only Garry had his grandad's message; there was a key, a decorative quartz stone at the side of the fireplace which blushed in the firelight because of the secret it was holding. When gently turned to the right it released the huge, ponderous hearthstone, which turned on a finely poised axis to reveal the wonderland below. Everything necessary was there, including the 'worm', to produce Garry's special uisge beatha. The fumes crept up the chimney through the base of the fireplace to mingle with the frangrant, couthy tang of the peat.

To replace the hearthstone was simplicity itself. Garry had only to place his foot on the tilted edge and the massive stone swung back to neatly kiss the fireplace and be securely locked in place by the rose quartz stone.

But the quality of Garry's brew was far too good to remain in the obscurity of the valley and when word of it spread to the world outside, there were ears to listen.

One afternoon, when the robin was singing its little skirling song as a requiem to the dying year and the first snow flakes floated down from the gathering clouds the Excise Officer and his henchmen made a lightning raid on Garry's croft. They found him half asleep and dreaming by the fireside in his favourite rocking chair, half a gallon of 'the best' by his side.

There were three of them, bursting through the door waving a warrant paper to prove their right. The officer in charge turned to his two companions and gave the peremptory order,

"Search the house".

When the two men had left the room, Garry and the officer

studied each other carefully, a glint of recognition lighting up their eyes. Not a word was said. As the the two searchers returned the officer, by chance, tapped the fireplace with his stick. There was a hollow echo.

"Nothing here!", the men reported.

"Right", said their leader, "we'll be off then. But, MacDonald, this practice will have to cease" and, with a twinkle in his eye, he moved towards the door.

Garry drew himself up smartly and saluted.

"Yes, surr", he said.

Once outside, the first lieutenant questioned his superior.

"Why did you not lift that hearthstone?" And the officer, with a faraway look in his eyes, replied,

"That fellow did me a very, very good turn. And", resuming his authoritative tone, continued, "we have no evidence".

Garry had felt the depth of emotion between the two men, accepted the advice and set about putting his neglected croft in order and, regretfully, informed the community that he had gone out of business and his 'supplies' must cease.

A neighbour, noted for his fondness of a good dram, took the news very badly. When the hens had been shut in and he had checked the sow for signs of farrowing, and seen the pony snugly stabled, he would look over the Tummel valley on a night when the harvest moon was admiring her reflection in the placid waters of the loch and sniffing the air mutter enviously:

"Garry is making a drop for himself tonight".

Fingal, the fox and Hector, the hound were the two one called upon when facing the kind of trouble they specialised in dealing with.

One warm, sunny day, Irralee and I found ourselves plunged into just that kind of trouble. We were seated at the table for our mid-day meal when we were interrupted by the screams of the cockerel. They were his last. He was the first to die, flying in the face of the attackers to protect his flock from a pack of marauding foxes.

Wishing we were dreaming, we counted the dazed survivors. We had lost ten hens and the cockerel in a matter of minutes. All that was left was a trail of feathers clinging to the grass in a last pathetic, almost apologetic, message left by the victims. There was the body of a lovely young pullet, unmarked, unruffled which had simply died of fright.

This was something I had never met before — mass murder in broad daylight. I filled my cartridge belt and strapped it on in a smouldering rage, slipped the tiny impassive bullets into the cavity of the Winchester rifle, slung it across my shoulder and picked up my shotgun. There must be bodies somewhere that the raiders would return to collect and I hoped to be at the meeting place. Lying in the field next to the croft on the west, from where I suspected the foxes had come, the pains of cramp came over me but I knew to move now was to betray my presence.

A drumming of hooves suddenly found me surrounded by cattle. They were all panting and clooted in the sweating of distress, their staring eyes trying desperately to speak. I saw, in an instant, the cause of their trouble, it was a large, despicable warble fly. It floated menacingly around the herd its one desire to penetrate the skins and leave its hide-boring progeny. The monster fly landed on Drumbuie's broad back. That was good, he was the canny one, and I rose and smote the warble fly with my hand, apologising, at the same time, to my friend. He took it stoically and there was an immediate sense of peace as the broken body of the warble fell to the ground.

I lay on my back in the grass and the cattle gathered around and blotted out the sky with their great, hairy heads. They snuffed and snorted with big, moist muzzles and no greater thanks could ever be given. Rising I made my way back towards the house, stopping for a moment to pick a mushroom.

Looking up again I saw a large dog fox boldly stalking through the field with a pullet in his mouth. He hadn't seen me and looked surprised when he did. I shot him but was very uneasy, as one fox could not have wrought all that death and destruction.

I was right. They struck again next day just after the hens had been released, with the resulting loss of six, and again in the afternoon. I was sure they must be a pack of about twenty strong, well equipped with the cunning of their kind knowing to lie low when the man smell was in the air, with their hungry bellies knotted to the ground, but when the air cleared to move in for the slaughter.

Irralee was in the stable in the afternoon fussing over her filly which, after a caper around Creag Mhor, was lame on her near fore leg. Hearing a commotion among the hens, Irralee dashed out and met a fox, face to face, with a pullet in its mouth. Startled, with its escape route cut off, the fox, a full grown cub but inexperienced, hesitated.

She screamed at it, and when Irralee screams at anything it has to pay attention. The fox was petrified and made off, still clutching its prize. But Irralee is very, very fleet of foot and was in hot pursuit, screaming and making valiant snatches at the fox's brush. This was too much for Reynard which leapt into a nearby blackthorn bush. Irralee flung herself after it and they faced up to each other, in the scratching, tearing bush, snarling.

But Irralee always keeps her best scream to the last and she let it go full in the fox's face, yelling,

"Murderer".

That, as far as the fox was concerned, was more than enough. It dropped its victim and fled.

Crawling back out of the blackthorn Irralee stroked the pullet's feathers into place, cleaned up the bird's blood with her hankie and took it home. This pullet recovered and eventually was able to recount to her chicks how she had been snatched from the jaws of death.

Irralee fed me the full account, machine-gun fashion. I reached for the phone and Fingal, the Fox, promised immediate action. He would contact Hector, the Hound, that night, then raise a posse of rifles. He phoned us that night to stable the horses as the hounds would be there at dawn.

The menace from this plague of foxes had been building up over the years and the afforestation of the highlands had given them the shelter they had always yearned for. In the dense cover of the fir trees, where the protection was such that not even the raindrops penetrated, they bred and multiplied, with no need to burrow into the ground for an earth. The vixens made cosy nests in the deep pine needles and suckled their cubs in a security beyond their wildest dreams.

And so the valley quickly ran out of its wild birds, rabbits and hares and the bandits had turned their attention to Croft Douglas and its easy-to-catch chicken suppers.

At first light next morning there was the first, distant, eerie howl that increased in a thunderous crescendo. Nothing seems to strike more fear and terror into wild animals, and humans forbye, than the baying of the hounds in full cry. Their quarry has everything to fear and we could hear them coming nearer and nearer, their cries rising in pitch as they approached their kill.

The foxes fled before them to meet the merciful crack and spit of guns lying concealed in the heather and bracken. They picked off the foxes as they raced towards them. There were no wasted bullets here; these men were all crackshots, gamekeepers, stalkers, gillies, farmers and farmers' sons who, proud of their skill with the rifle and, for a ploy like this, would cheerfully leave the warmth of their beds behind; men from Dalnacardoch, Blair Atholl, Killiecrankie, Pitlochry and Strathtay, who lay in ambush, linked together by walkie-talkie sets, in a line across Creag Mhor, between the foxes and their home in the forest.

It was the day of reckoning for the foxes. How often, in their raids, had they revelled in the fiendish delight of striking terror into the hearts of their victims, before chopping them up in their powerful jaws. Now, with the tables turned, it was they who shivered at the hellish baying of the hounds and were, in turn, overcome by the spectre of fear, which paused only long enough to tie knots in their insides.

The last year's cubs, fat and well grown, which had known only the good life, fell first. The older ones, more experienced, hugged the cover and thought, desperately of an avenue of escape. It would take a cunning one, indeed, to escape this morning.

Thirteen foxes were claimed by the rifles.

It was over and, one by one, they rose from their hiding places in the bracken, boulders and heather and stretched their cramped limbs. The men were in jubilant mood and made their way down to the Loch Tummel hotel where there had been arranged a large dram and a steaming bowl of leek and tattie soup for all. In the distance, Hector's hunting horn could still be heard calling his scattered pack of hounds together, so we kept Hector's dram cold and his soup hot.

We could hear the long drawn-out coaxing note, blown so expertly, notes that promised the hounds a paradise of meaty bones. They just could not resist this tempting call to the hungry, and hounds are always hungry. So back they came, in ones and twos, and were loaded into the van, which set off for Strathtay and the promised meal.

The sharpshooters were making their way back to their homes and various places of work, to the jobs that had waited a bit longer than usual but still were to be done.

I was on the point of leaving myself when I heard a hair-raising, piercing scream and a lady sped past me, showing more than a normal turn of speed. Following, and desperately trying to catch up, was mine host, MacKenzie, shouting,

"It will be all right", but, in the passing, he gasped out of the side of his mouth,

"Gideon, how do you deal with an adder?"

It was the last thing I expected. I hadn't come across an adder for a very long time and never in a hotel! But it was there, all right, inside the doorway.

The lady, a newly arrived guest looking for Reception had found one, and it had greatly shaken her.

I gazed at the snake and knew immediately that this was going to be no case of 'shoo-ing' it away. It was a big one, a 'king adder' and, effortlessly and contemptuously, it disengaged another couple of coils to rise higher and fix me with his bright, round, unblinking beady eyes. I gazed coldly back. The forked tongue, flicking in and out, was the only movement and now I had to move as swiftly as that.

Without unlocking eyes I, ever so slowly, slid my sgian dhubh from its sheath in my stocking. The edge of my blade I always kept sharp and the snake never knew who won the 'strike'. There was a protracted 'Aah' from the onlookers, who stood at a respectable distance around the porch.

I had read about the mongoose and the cobra and felt a deep sense of satisfaction that I, too, had matched speed of movement with a snake.

When skinned out it was a trophy to remind me that this had been no dream, but reality.

25

It was time for a change of bull, our present one would soon be coming round to his own stock and a father cavorting with his own daughters was something that would scandalize the cattle world. Whilst we were debating, discussing the exchequer and doing lots of sums on scraps of paper about the possibility of buying another bull, I met a man at the market.

I had never met this man before, but he possessed a herd of Highland cattle and proudly announced himself as owner of the bull that had won this year's championship at Oban. I was impressed and confided that I was, at the moment, looking for a Highland bull. My new found friend seemed to be slowly digesting this and, in the meantime, steered me in the direction of the market bar.

After three nips of whisky and three glasses of beer, he slapped his hand on the bar counter and solemnly announced,

"I am liking you and am going to do you a favour". He paused for another deep sip and slid the back of his hand across his mouth. "I am finished with Victor for this year. You can have him for the rest of the summer".

Cautiously, I asked, "How much?"

My new friend leaned towards me, breathing the fumes of his last drink full in my face and said, in a conspiritorial whisper that held the tones of one making a colossal sacrifice.

"Just get the next drink and you can have the bull for the price of the transport and the grazing of him".

I couldn't believe my luck; the services of a champion bull just for the cost of floating him and the grass he would eat! I dug into my sporran, bought the drinks and shook hands on the deal.

The very next day Victor arrived, accompanied by his owner who, after consuming half a bottle of whisky I had specially purchased for the occasion, confided that the bull could be 'a little cantankerous'. I had a good look at Victor. He was a brindle, with stripes so dark and so golden that intermixed with every movement of his massive shoulders. He was also huge, and I was to be his keeper. I shuddered inside.

I was not unused to the weight of responsibility, but around half a ton of bone and muscle, with doubtful temperament, was, indeed, a heavy load. I have always believed that, in animals and humans alike, the eye is the mirror of its owner's mind. Victor, so far, had only spared a cursory glance in my direction. I didn't know what his thoughts were, but I thought I had never seen an eye so mean, so deadly mean.

In spite of my misgivings, Victor settled down peacefully with the herd and set about his business of 'being boss' and keeping the cows contented when the need arose and the pleasant summer days wended their way tranquilly to the sound of the munching of the season's gift of the luscious grass and red and white clovers, the author of many a contented belch.

They were happy, lazy, sultry days and Victor had finished his courtships. This, in time, left the big bull feeling more than a bit restless and, when he heard a heifer's call in a neighbouring herd to the west, he strolled through all the barriers as if they never existed. The fence wires parted, and the stone dykes collapsed before his massive chest. Next, he demolished the Angus bull, which was preparing to attend to the heifer, and attended to her himself.

The owner of the heifer could not have been more understanding. Together we examined his bull and decided it would live for another day. But what to do about the heifer? Her owner was an 'Angus' man and wasn't at all enthusiastic about a Highland x Angus calf. There was only one thing for it. I rang the vet immediately, and he arrived complete with the equipment necessary to annul the illicit love affair. If Victor, I thought, is going to carry on in this fashion it could become very expensive, so I kept a tight eye on him from the moment he woke until, with a series of deep grunts, he bedded down. But, I knew, that in his idleness he was getting more and more tied up with himself, more morose and, worst of all, meaner.

The crisis came one sunny morning. Irralee, Shona and I had gone down to the lochside to inspect a section of fencing that was in danger of subsiding in surrender to the onslaught of the water. Its waves, from the south-west, were biting deeply at the earth of the bank.

On the way down to the loch I had been joking about the bull chasing us and was reassured, with equal hilarity, that we could all outrun him. The joke quickly died when Victor suddenly appeared with an earsplitting roar, showing us he was in the mood to exterminate everything, and everybody, from the face of the earth. The ground shook as he dug in his threatening feet, savagely tossing the clods over his shoulder, and charged!

It was a case of 'women and children first' and I yelled, "Clear out. It's the bull".

They needed no second bidding. They were off and so was I, bringing up the rear, with the thunder of the bull's hooves rumbling in my ears. Running blindly, we headed straight into a bog. The sucking mud gripped our feet and with the heavy drag on every footstep the bull was steadily gaining on us. I could feel his hot breath behind me and turned to see his enormous head only a few feet away. I roared back at him with all the breath I could find. He stopped in his tracks,

which proved to be his undoing, as his great weight took him firmly down into the bog.

Shona and Irralee were clear of the bog by now and watched me anxiously as I made for firmer ground. Looking back I saw Victor pull his feet slowly out of the gripping bog. He had had enough and, for me, I had had my fill, too, and was at the end of the road in my journey with Victor.

I rang his owner that night to tell him his bull would be on his way home in the morning. But how to do it? How to get him loaded into a cattle truck? I would need reinforcements.

That night I made my way to the Tummel Hotel. Angus was there all right; from the open doorway I could hear him at his story telling about an eagle he had seen, high above the moor, quartering every yard of the ground.

"Yon birdie", he said, "must have been starving after days and days of poor hunting", and he paused to swallow his dram, "for he would never have done what he did. He had spied a fox fast asleep, as fast asleep as a fox can get, curled up snugly in a bed of heather, and swept in, striking the fox a tremendous blow as he grabbed him in his talons. Straining every muscle he rose to a full twelve feet above the ground, but the fox, an old dog with many escapades behind him suddenly awakened from his nightmare and, twisting his head, took a quick bite at the eagle's leg.

This was too much for the big bird and he let go. The fox dropped with a thump to the ground and ran all the way, yelping, to his den and the eagle rose higher and higher, with only a few tufts of red hair sticking to his talons."

Angus looked round the company "Yon must have been a fell hungry birdie". Then he spotted me.

"Feasgar math. Thig a stigh, mo charaid, and haff a dram." He always spoke this way after his third dram. I drew in my chair to join the company.

"Angus", I said, "your story reminds me that I saw something today for the first time ever, an osprey on Loch Tummel."

"Well, well, now, look at that", said Angus. "I never did see that either."

"He was there all right, probably with a hen and two chicks awaiting his return home."

And he was a long way from home, most likely from the Loch of the Lowes and, having frightened the fish for miles around his eyrie, decided to give Loch Tummel a trial.

So graceful in flight, circling, ever circling with his crested head bent to scan the water, with eyes that held the best sight in the world. Just a quiver of his body would show that he had spotted his quarry. Down, down he went with the wind shrieking through his pinions, with talons outspread, he hit the water and it lifted to engulf him. But, like a cork, he bounced back to the surface, his wings beating wildly, flailing the surface of the water mercilessly as he gradually rose with a huge, brown trout grasped just behind the dorsal fin in his right foot. It was a big fish and the lift away was laborious but, by degrees, the osprey took control and his left foot changed grip to stop the fish flapping. So, with a wriggling, head down dip to the water the fish said a last farewell to Loch Tummel.

Angus was impressed.

"Man," he said, "I would surely like to haff seen that but, I tell you, I saw a kestrel on the hunt, hanging in the sky like a pinned butterfly, and down he went and came up clutching a large 'puddock' by the hind leg. It wriggled this way and that and took the kestrel on the most turbulent flight of its life. Oho", gurgled Angus "it was a highland frog, wass that one."

He stopped for a regretful pause before resuming, "I neffer did see the finish but," he brightened up, "I think it must have been a French kestrel with a liking for frogs. Eech, eech, eech!"

When Angus tried to contain his laughter his body shook uncontrollably, the table rocked and everything in the room rattled. The situation slowly returned to something approximating normal and I came to the reason for my presence.

"Angus," I said, "I have a problem with a bull."

Angus sat bolt upright in his chair. "Well, look at that, now. I haff a bull on my mind, too."

I took a look at Angus' broad brow and thought the animal had plenty of room. It transpired that Angus had to borrow a bull and it was ready for returning and, there and then, we made a pact with each other to help despatch them.

Next morning Angus came chugging up the hill in his Land Rover, encouraging it up the braes with exorbitant pushes on the steering wheel.

"Well, now," said Angus, "I was late and came without my breakfast," which was a broad hint for someone to put a pan of something on somewhere. "But," he added, "I see you have him penned already."

And, I had, indeed, with more than a bit of trouble, and cunning and a trail of turnips, lured Victor into the loading pens at the roadside and there he was, chumping the lumps of turnip down as though they were so many peas.

"I thought," I said to Angus, "if I bogged him down with turnips he might be quieter."

"That was good thinking."

"Yes," I replied, "I was thinking it was good thinking."

The float arrived and backed up to the loading pens with a fussy shuffle of its tyres. As the ramp came down Victor made it quite plain he intended to have no part in this and treated us to what was meant to be a series of intimidating snorts as he turned his head towards me. I slipped an arm through the rails of the pen and quickly snicked a humbug onto Victor's big, broad nose. This action met with a blood-curdling roar of disapproval, but, at least, he was now under some sort of control and I joined the bull in the pen, with a tug at the lead rope I tried to remind him who was boss.

I started to lead the way up the ramp and Angus heaved his great bulk to give support to the rear and Victor, mean to the last, gathered his shaggy hind leg for an immediate delivery. Angus, sensing the coming blow, birled round and took the kick on his broad backside. It was a powerful whack that would have felled many a man, but Angus only 'groo-ed' for a moment, then went in to the attack. As I pulled the leading rope he seized the bull by the tail and gave it an almighty twist then, putting his shoulder and all of his eighteen stone, propelled him into the float.

My escape was through a small door in the front, with the hot smell of bull's breath strong in my nostrils. The float clasped its jaws tightly to avoid any thought of retreat on the bull's part, gave a hiss of satisfaction as the tight hold of the brakes was released and trundled on its way. Inside, Victor gave a last mournful bellow of farewell but, at Croft Douglas, every eye was dry at the parting.

The next morning dawned with the second half of the bargain. The bull Angus had on loan was a finely marked red roan Shorthorn, not as massive as Victor, and with an eye that said he would be a lot easier to deal with. But there was no float this time and, answering my questioning glances, Angus informed me he was only going to a croft this side of Struan.

"There's a short cut over the hill," he said, "and this will save the 'floating' money and," he added with a chuckle "we can spend that on the uisge-beatha." He followed this with a dig from his outsized elbow which I just managed to dodge and save myself some possible damage.

It was a beautiful morning, the skylarks were bouncing up, tiny feathered rockets shooting into the blue, with an unhurried ascent and time to sing all the way. I thought, how varied were the voices of the birds and the lark was surely one of the sweetest and fully deserved that spot in the heavens which every day he strove, time after time, to reach.

We plodded on up the steepness of the hill. There was no breath to spare for idle conversation, not like the villainous voices of the hoodie crows. Two of them, perched high on the top of a 'roundel' of silver spruce, were conversing about the finding of a dead sheep.

"I saw a hoggie, deid," croaked one.

"Whaur, oh whaur?" screeched the other.

A cock red grouse jumped up in front of us. He had the

stern voice of authority and bid us 'Go back, go back' and, as we reached the crest of the moor, there came the never-to-be-forgotten call of the whaup; the soft, rounded, liquid notes 'Curlee, curlee'. If these were, indeed, the lost souls of people, they were not unhappy, not like the gulls wheeling over the lochan we were passing. I was sure they must be the souls of misers, snatched away from their gold.

My musing received a severe jolt in the shape of a vicious butt from the bull which landed me in a moist bed of sphagnum moss. Angus looked over the top of the animal and said, in tones of concern,

"Was he dunking you, then?"

Dunking me! I felt as if my left ribcage had been stoved in, but staggered up to my feet, regained a hold on the halter and resolved to pay more attention for the rest of the journey.

The bull raised his head and sniffed the air, the distant smell of home was filtering in to his nostrils. It only needed the faint, exciting call of one of his females to put him into a trot. Angus and I were left with no option but to break into a trot, too.

It couldn't last. Angus was the first to go down and his generous body ploughed great furrows through the heather as he was towed along. Soon, it was my turn to fall. This, I thought, with Angus' weight on the other side, must halt the bull. Not a bit. The voice he was hearing was surely the soft, seductive bellow of his favourite wife and, coming through the heather and the myrtle and the moss in my face, I heard Angus' anguished cry.

"Let the booger go." And we did.

Bedraggled and prone, and without a vestige of breath in our bodies, we silently watched the bull's heels vanish into the distance. Angus got his voice back first.

"Well, well, look at that, now," he said. "Are we not the lucky ones? That's a good five miles we've saved the walking of."

"Lucky!" I thought, inspecting myself with the wonder that I was still all in one piece.

"Yes, yes," reiterated Angus. "We are the lucky ones. Let's turn for home."

The word 'home' and the soft way he said it never sounded so sweet. We parted with a shake of the hands at the top of Creag Mhor.

This is the point where the whole of the Tummel valley lies at your feet. It matters not how often you see it, it is always breathtaking with Schiehallion holding court at the top of the loch and the other purple-clad peaks in attendance; Meall Tarruin chon, Farragon, Creag an Loch, Creag Dhubh and Beinn Eagach and there, floating in the sky, an osprey, back for another Tummel trout.

Some wonder why this bird flies from the warmth of the African sun, hundreds of hazardous miles to mate and rear its family in the highlands of Scotland.

It's no wonder to me!